Teachers in Nomadic Spaces

OMPLICATED

CONVERSATION

A Book Series
of Curriculum
Studies

William F. Pinar
General Editor

Vol. 5

PETER LANG
New York • Washington, D.C./Baltimore • Bern
Frankfurt am Main • Berlin • Brussels • Vienna • Oxford

Kaustuv Roy

Teachers in Nomadic Spaces

Deleuze and Curriculum

PETER LANG
New York • Washington, D.C./Baltimore • Bern
Frankfurt am Main • Berlin • Brussels • Vienna • Oxford

Library of Congress Cataloging-in-Publication Data

Roy, Kaustuv.
Teachers in nomadic spaces: Deleuze and curriculum /
Kaustuv Roy.
p. cm. — (Complicated conversation; vol. 5)
Includes bibliographical references (p.).
1. Deleuze, Gilles—Contributions in education. 2. Education—Philosophy.
3. Postmodernism and education. 4. Curriculum change.
5. Teacher-student relationships. I. Title. II. Series.
LB880.D4362R69   370'.1—dc21   2002154662
ISBN 0-8204-6737-5
ISSN 1534-2816

Bibliographic information published by **Die Deutsche Bibliothek**.
Die Deutsche Bibliothek lists this publication in the "Deutsche
Nationalbibliografie"; detailed bibliographic data is available
on the Internet at http://dnb.ddb.de/.

Cover design by Lisa Barfield

The paper in this book meets the guidelines for permanence and durability
of the Committee on Production Guidelines for Book Longevity
of the Council of Library Resources.

© 2003 Peter Lang Publishing, Inc., New York
275 Seventh Avenue, 28th Floor, New York, NY 10001
www.peterlangusa.com

Printed in the United States of America

Contents

Preface

What does it mean to think again, deeply to reconsider something? For Deleuze, it is not simply the having of another thought or another idea; instead, it is the very reinstatement of difference in thought: "that profound fracture" by which thought can access the "genitality" of thinking. And this is at the same time incessant practice. In conversation with Michel Foucault Deleuze once said, "No theory can develop without eventually encountering a wall," and the only way to "pierce this wall" is through practice. This book presents elements of that wall through which are dragged Deleuzian "tensors" to produce an altered *skapos* and fresh oscillations. The inability to *think* difference in most institutional settings makes such attempts at transformation crucial. This is especially so in colonized spaces of which the urban school setting is a prime example. Deleuzian concepts place us in a transformational matrix, a space of potential difference through which passes, from time to time, a spike of lightning that is the active realization of the transformative power of life. Each concept shatters existing modes of thinking about the everyday. Brought to bear on the conditions of schooling, they allow us to access sudden breathless hollows that can make curriculum swerve from the old terrain. And what is surprising is that this does not call for grand movements or breaks, nor for great reforms, but depends on the subversive power of the very small and minor "flections"; secret lines of disorientation. The change that is the result is neither structural nor individual, but consists of fresh embodiments of a subpersonal kind: blocks of intensities that have the potential to change curricular relations within an immanent field. This book is an experiment toward such a change, invoking Deleuze in the midst of an empirical series to open up a new conversation.

Introduction

Fieldwork in Theory

A thing, an animal, a person are only definable by movements and rests, speeds and slownesses, and by affects and intensities.
——Gilles Deleuze, *Dialogues*

Most truths are less interesting than the complex and dynamic intercrossing of forces, intensities, discourses, desires, accidents, idiosyncrasies, and relations of power that produce those culminations. For these networks, while revealing the bifurcations and determinations, the choices, impulses, and propensities, en-route to a particular set of distillations, cannot fail to indicate at the same time unactualized possibilities, fields of indefinitude, and lines of escape.

As found in the writings of the Frankfurt School, the term *praxis* has meant, roughly, a transformative mode of perception-in-action (Vázquez, 1977, 133). I will use the term here to indicate an effort to reconstellate sense data, propelling us toward a reinsertion of our identities and practices that are reciprocally determined in such indefinite networks as above, in the flows and unformed intensities beneath systems of articulation in the social field, with a view not to recover any essence or discover any truth, but to open up the fastnesses in which thought takes refuge, provoking by that same parting novel, nonhumanist stirrings.

The present study is praxeological in this sense. Although its starting point is a case study, the work is not wholly or even largely empirical. One can describe it in terms of what Pierre Bourdieu (1990) has called "fieldwork in philosophy." That is to say, it is an effort to employ empirical work in directly engaging theoretical and philosophical issues in order to achieve a reinsertion into the morphogenic processes at the intersections of which arise events and phenomena. Expressed in other words, it makes philosophy go to work for us amid the turmoil of the everyday and attunes us to a different kind of observation or angle of vision that renders visible what was not previously apparent. The theory that I engage here for this purpose is the philosophy and social theory of Gilles Deleuze, the philosopher of difference, for whom the important thing has always been not solutions, but to pose a problem so as to open up worlds.

In broad terms, there are two different series involved in this study—one empirical and the other conceptual. The primary effort here is to set up a resonance between the two in order that expressional flashes can occur between the two series creating summarily breaches for action. The empirical part pertains to teacher induction and formation under urban conditions, and is based on observations, discussions, and dialogues with novice teachers in an urban innovative school. Against the imperatives of the terrain the teachers needed to negotiate, I examine the concepts, categories, implicit assumptions, significations, and boundary distinctions on which they leaned in order to approach, and make sense of, those spaces. To put it in another way, I observed the category constructs through which the novice teachers approached the "known," in this case the pedagogic context, and the complex ways in which those constructs contributed to the difficulties they encountered in the urban situation. For it is accurate to say from the perspective of this study that "to know is to produce in thought, and the production reconstitutes the way in which phenomena are produced" (Piaget cited in von Glasersfeld, 1987, 110). The pragmatic purpose was to introduce a "swerve" or a deviation in the plane of taken-for-granted assumptions by means of which a new experiment in thought could be inserted in the interstices that might help teachers get an insight into the generative possibilities of the situation.

The necessity for producing that swerve ushers in the conceptual part. Dissatisfied with the general thrust of mainstream teacher education that rarely considers the complex ambiguities of irregular spaces, and prefers to raise issues in terms of limiting and worn-out representations and categories—accountability, professionalization, efficiency, to name a few—I reconstitute the spaces that I observed using a different cartography. My intention was to initiate a plane of intensities and becomings rather than recuperation and representation, new relays and formations instead of the structure of categories and boundaries that has dominated mainstream practices.[1] For the question was, how can we get out of the cycle of stagnant reproductions that produce "self-reflective homologies" and instead, "rejoin a continuum of potential." In other words, the question was "how to perform an atypical expression capable of diverting the process into rebecoming" (Massumi, 2002, xxvi). In pursuit of such ontogenetic possibilities, that is, emergent relations of force rather than fixed categories, I propose here a conceptual framework that might allow us to array ourselves differently, and consider the new set of subjective acts that must be carried out when confronted with the problem of reintensification.

Attempting such a praxis, the book addresses itself to teacher educators, curriculum theorists, practicing teachers, and to those interested in differential spaces and urban issues, urging us into a different kind of vectoring of sense-intensities than is afforded in conventional approaches to teacher education and curriculum practice. The pragmatics of such an effort involves the generation of new intervals that are sprouted by means of experimentation through inserting existing strata or bound qualities into Deleuzian concepts that act as circuits of "micro-agitations," or infinitesimal movements of displacement, leading to a freedom for alternative deployments in intervals that are "anexact and yet rigorous."[2] The reader must be warned that this is not a book about "fixing" anything or about providing quick solutions. Instead, it invites the reader to enter into an experimental mode and work through the contents of these pages so as to become coextensive with the problem itself, enter its plane as it were, extending and radicalizing the horizon of possibilities in embodying it, discovering new chromatic variations in the process of such a meditation. For a true problem, according to Deleuze, is never fully solved, but persists despite solutions in the infinite play of desire, thereby retaining its problematicity.

Known as the "philosopher of the city,"[3] Deleuze, along with Felix Guattari, investigated the architectonics of urbanity, which makes this analysis particularly relevant, as it brings to bear Deleuzian distinctions or differential formations on the learning spaces of an inner-city school, working out a different way of looking. Deleuze saw the city as unleashing forces that are not fully captured or controlled by the machinery of the State—ephemeral forces of an irruptive kind with the power of metamorphosis. Seen through this lens, the complex and turbulent conditions of urban or inner-city schooling yield a somewhat different subtext, and offer a glimmer of possibilities that might serve the irreducible multiplicity of the student populace better than most of the modernist mainstream educational policies and practices in which they are imbricated (Giroux, 2000).

Seen through a Deleuzian lens, a curriculum that follows narrow goals, that attempts to homogenize and limit the signs and processes of learning, for example, to functioning within representationalist ideologies and specific needs such as those of the market, denying in the process difference and complex multiplicity, runs the risk of locking us into increasingly oppressive grids. For implicit in such a view of curriculum is the assumption of the "world as icon," or the insistence of a unified reality that we must jointly hold and serve. But as Nietzsche and a succession of other thinkers have argued, there is *no such world*. Turning Plato's famous cave allegory on its head, Nietzsche wrote: "behind each cave [there is] another that opens still more deeply, and beyond each surface a subterranean world yet more vast, more strange...under every ground, a subsoil more profound" (cited in Deleuze, 1990b, 263). This gives an endlessly multiplicitous and divergent picture of the "world" that gets subsumed and totalized in the convergent views of mainstream curriculum practice, resulting in a cutting off from the field of potentialities that inhere in difference.

The environment I discuss demanded a different response from teachers in terms of what could unfold as learning opportunities, and how these could be successfully identified under volatile conditions. Although the school itself was open to innovation, the beginning teachers I encountered were ill-equipped conceptually to countenance these divergent forces, and continued to be bound by the Platonic tenets of "image-copy," or recognition and representation, that defines so much of schoolwork.[4] The teacher education programs some of these neophytes had been through had not helped them to see the generative possibilities of irregular spaces, nor were the usual professional development programs, aimed more at the normative compulsions of mainstream schools, of much use here.

Ill-equipped to see difference in terms of its pedagogical potential, these beginning teachers struggled to cope in a highly differentiated atmosphere, with the result that they experienced considerable difficulties, friction, and stress. In other words, their training was at odds with the demands of the context. Observing this, it seemed to me that teacher preparation deserved a different kind of theoretical attention that would not merely seek regularities and order, but be able to see learning opportunities in irregular spaces and moments, and in discontinuous flashes rather than in continuities. The supple force of Deleuzian pragmatics that sees difference, and not similarity, as the driving force in processes of becoming, seemed particularly apt for working out the pragmatics of this alternative vision.

Therefore, a basic conceptual shift seemed necessary that would prepare beginning teachers to embrace the constructive possibilities of positive difference. For as I saw it, the learning spaces and pedagogical possibilities often were where the teachers were not. It also appeared to me that it was not a mere question of adding one more pedagogic dimension to the teachers' repertoire; instead it connected to the very images teachers held of themselves and their roles that reified the boundaries and limited possibilities of action. By means of a theoretical effort of reconceptualization, I hoped to open up these images in thought, with a view to offering a pragmatics of reconstruction that would be dynamic and engage many more levels than currently possible.

I saw the task as, first, theorizing the character of the spaces I was observing in the school, and the pedagogical possibilities that these held. Second, I viewed it as formulating certain conceptual tools for ways of looking, thinking, and experimenting so that through the operationalization or enactment of this new mode, the grip of the existing boundaries and categories that are the result of settled dispositions could be loosened, as well as the means worked out for realizing the pedagogical possibilities of irregular spaces.

And since dispositions cannot be isolated from the notion of individuality, these could not be opened up without an examination of the notion of identity and affect that is woven into them (Pinar, 1994, 1998). Therefore it was important to look at certain affective investments of teachers as well, for which purpose I chose to look at the occurrence of stress as a critical existential phenomenon among teachers that arose from the way in which the urban situation affected them and was an important indicator of it. In sum, these provided contact with thought-affect networks where ideas of self and curriculum are reproduced, and into the interstitial spaces of which one could insert operations that might provoke a new intensity. But before moving on, let us take a brief look at the empirical background of the study and the conditions surrounding it.

Induction and Retention
First, the problem of teacher induction and retention is a serious issue not just in innovative environs but in school systems throughout the United States. S. Eileen and Stephen Weiss (1999) observe:

> Over two million new K-12 teachers will be employed in the U.S. over the next decade…more than one-third of these new teachers will be hired in low wealth *urban and rural school districts*. This large population of new teachers will be challenged to educate diverse learners in an increasingly complex [situation]. Unfortunately first-year teachers are frequently left in a "sink or swim" position with little support from colleagues and few opportunities for professional development. Well-organized induction programs are the exception rather than the rule, and haphazard induction experiences have been associated with higher levels of attrition as well as lower levels of teacher effectiveness. Current estimates are that more than 20% of public school teachers leave their positions within three years. (4) (emphasis added)

This means that out of the total estimated number of fresh inductees mentioned above, more than four hundred thousand will leave their jobs in the initial years. This, by all accounts, is an alarming rate of attrition.

Further, among those who choose to remain in the profession, large numbers—in some districts up to 40 percent—leave the urban settings to teach in suburban school districts (Weiss, 1999). This problem of 'flight' among teachers is attributable in part to teachers' lack of experience and understanding of the social and economic context of the students, that is, of the problem of difference. But school districts, reading the problem in terms of control and classroom management issues, have attempted to solve the problem of both teacher flight and low student achievement by referring 'problem' students to alternative schools or programs or by referring them to special education (Sanders, 2000).

However, this system of winnowing and sifting students does little to resolve critical questions surrounding the becoming and formation of teachers who will teach in urban settings, and to determine how best to construct a viable education for students in such settings. Instead, this approach simply results in the undesirable formation of school tiers according to student skill levels, student compliance, and teacher coping abilities. And that is merely to deflect the issue to an alternative site, not to deal with it. It leads to another kind of segregation.

An adequate response lies not in categorizing students and putting them away in special education sites, but in finding ways to help teachers teach different students differently by reconsidering existing assumptions of what constitutes teaching and learning that binds them to the Same. It was apparent to me that this was not an issue of systemic reform that could be fixed by making large-scale structural changes, but rather, a question of basic perceptions about education, and the boundaries and categories employed in thinking about school and curriculum.

Of course, not all of the problem of teacher flight or attrition can be attributed to problems of inadequate induction processes, but studies (National Commission on Teaching and America's Future, 1996) show that it plays a significant role in the loss of teachers. Reports also show that better induction programs keep teachers from leaving. This makes teacher induction a vital area of concern and study. Its importance is also heightened by the fact that "it is a boundary spanning field, connecting teacher education, teaching conditions in the schools, and field based professional development" (Olebe, 2001, 71). There are often interesting problems at the edges and interfaces of these adjoining fields because the interfacing is not always smooth, and the edges often do not mesh. These result in odd boundary conditions that have generative possibilities. In other words, there are interstices and irregular spaces that can be explored. Eileen and Stephen Weiss (1999) have also noted that, despite the positive impact of induction programs on retention rates, there has been little sustained commitment in recent years to permanently institute teacher induction programs as part of a formal entry process into the field. New teachers have been left to figure things out once they get into the classroom. An inadvertent consequence of this has been the tendency on the part of teachers to reproduce the existing patterns in a desperate bid for survival.

Britzman (1986) and others have shown how young teachers coming in with new ideas rarely have the room to exercise them or know how to bring together theory and practice. This is borne out by my own research and experience as a teacher educator. Further, this tension is all the more heightened in the urban classroom, where the old formulas of classroom management, a uniform curriculum, and standardized assessments fail to work as they fail to respond to the hugely complex and often racially marginalized lives of urban adolescents whose differences have been subsumed by a largely inflexible education system that operates with liberal majoritarian assumptions.

As the study proceeded, it became clear to me that the problem I was looking at was not merely one of teacher becoming and induction, but could be seen as part of a larger problem of teacher survival itself, in the context of increasing complexity of urban education, and the challenges posed by a student body who could by no means be seen or treated as a homogeneous group, and whose needs were so diverse that the very assumptions of schooling, such as a uniform curriculum, set timings, and the classroom as the primary site of learning, were put to question. It appeared to me that the order of complexity the teachers faced was not to be overcome merely through experience and "adjustment," or a matter of picking up certain "skills" on the job, but something that required a deeper shift in the conception of pedagogic relations, or a fundamental change in the way we think about learning, its content and expression, in order to free it from reification. That is to say, an effort at a much more fundamental level appeared to be necessary that would not merely amount to a reform of practice, but a reconfiguration of teacher being and becoming in an ever-shifting context.

Constitutive Difference

Often, the tensions that arose both in teachers and in the learning situation were the result of attempting to contain divergence within techno-managerial spaces, that is, within the horizons of possibility delineated by the teachers' own habits of thought, and the training they had received (see Liston and Zeichner, 1996). Not only did this subvert the innovative context, and result in important pedagogical opportunities being missed, but teachers admitted to feeling stressed, and expressed fears of early burnout through friction that the situation produced for them. A major statement made here is about the impossibility of dealing with difference from the perspective of unity. That is to say, to work positively with difference, we have to (find ways to) come to the realization that we ourselves are composed of difference, and that the thing we know as identity is at base a play of difference. It is then that a resonance occurs that breaks through identitarian ways of thinking.

What was necessary, therefore, was a new conceptual space in which the problem could be considered afresh, for new solutions sometimes require an altered theoretical *skupos* for their emergence. To give an example, problems which have remained unsolved for long periods of time, say, in algebra, sometimes have yielded solutions when restated in terms of geometry or topology. Likewise, a problem in clinical psychology is suddenly illuminated by looking at it from the perspective of communication theory (Bateson, 1991). My problem, as I began to formulate it, was to construct a conceptual frame that when entered into, or a praxis that when enacted, new teachers would be better able to insert themselves in differential spaces, as well as connect to creative fields of potential, avoiding the reduction of curriculum to identitarian ways of thinking. To put it differently, the problem was to formulate an immanent plane of expression that included the student, the teacher, and the curriculum that would aid in dehabituating us from frozen ways of thinking about the educational encounter itself, such as in the existing terms of what I will call a 'will-to-recognition' and a 'will-to-representation' that is discussed at length in the next chapter, and instead to grapple with the encounter from the perspective of a creative power of difference.

A Deleuzian Approach

What follows is a brief overview of the experimental framework that is appropriated for analysis of the case data, parts of which are further developed in each individual chapter. But let me remind the reader that the work is more of a looking into the possibilities of resonance between the two series, the empirical and the conceptual, than an interpretation. In this connection, Wolcott (1994) has written,

> More than simply linking up with theory or leaning on it for an interpretive framework, the objective here is to develop that framework. (43)

This is quite true in the case of the present study. Using the case as a transformational matrix, a loosely aggregated plane of the potential for innovative thinking in curriculum as well as the resistance to such change, of reification and emergence, of *difference and repetition*, I use Deleuzian concepts to help develop a different orientation in curriculum practice.

Fighting to retrieve philosophy from the oppressive weight of Hegelianism and the dialectic, Deleuze is an avowed empiricist or pluralist.[5] In line with thinkers such as Spinoza, Nietzsche, and Hume, Deleuze rejects all transcendent or idealist ground of experience. Universals do not explain anything, Deleuze is fond of saying, but must themselves be explained. And all explanation can only come from *within experience*, that is, from immanence, and not from an a priori, transcendental ground. There are no a priori Kantian categories that are the grounds of experience, but all universals are themselves the constructs of experience. Through the concept of immanence, Deleuze makes a relentless and intensive bid to overturn the transcendental idealism of Platonism. This means honoring difference and realizing its positivity.

But at the same time, does this mean reverting to the pre-Kantian deadlock between empiricism and idealism? The answer to that is a resounding no. Hidden in the earlier form of empiricism was the assumption of the experiencer as a sovereign humanistic agent. This created a confusion about how do "we," or humans, organize experience. It was a problem that could not be solved within the earlier form of empiricism. But it turned out to be a false problem. Nietzsche (1967) showed that "there is no 'being' behind doing...the deed is everything" (45). Radical empiricism contends that there is no experiencer or subject distinct from acts or experiences, but the notion of the experiencer itself comes out of the flow of experience. Immanence cannot have embedded in it a transcendental subject or a being who is outside the flow of experience.

What then is experience without the experiencer? It is nothing but sequences of contemplation and contraction, that is, observation and absorption like photosynthesis, or the formation of crystals, or the replication of nucleic acids and so on, none of which presupposes an agent, but the repetitious effects of which give rise to the illusion of a type of agency. Contractions built on contractions create layers or *strata* which harden to form the appearance of stable categories or agents. From the intensities and contractions that are infinitely strung out, certain patterns coagulate through insistent repetition due to previous constellations. The dog does not *possess* characteristics; out of the million intensities or possible traits of dogginess that exist as qualities and possible branchings emerges the dog. That is to say, the doglike traits that are themselves the result of infinitesimal contemplations are brought into proximity by vortices or attractors or resonances set up by previous contractions and contemplations. At no time is there an essence or the remote need for one. This is pure immanence that turns Platonism on its head.

What is the relevance of such a nonhumanist mode of thought and analysis to education that is seemingly a very humanistic enterprise? Before we can answer that question, one more clarification is necessary. Very broadly speaking, excessively categorical thinking can be maintained only at the expense of further becoming; strata upon strata generate forces that gravitate toward specific channels only. Over time, stringent orthodoxies appear that govern modes of being and thinking, along with rigid investments in maintaining the status quo. These tell us what should be, and what is acceptable or not acceptable, molding and shaping experience in highly selective ways. In other words, these adherences and allegiance to categories reify, strangling life and repeating old forms. It must be immediately clear that all forms of power and subjection must be predicated on ideas of "what must be," that is, from preset notions that shape experience, or what Deleuze and Guattari (1983b) call "signifier systems." These ideas or discourses do not belong to any particular agency but are the combined effects of myriad social forces that intersect to form despotic systems.

Education is one such system ruled by several regimes of signifiers—objective assessment, competence, risk, standardization, efficiency, to name a few, each a fallout of an earlier era of development in the so-called human sciences. Often the system seems to be in a viable mode to many as long as these slogans are repeated. These despotic signifiers look for the legitimation of their own self images, often resulting in the loss of other ways of looking, feeling and thinking, thus boxing up difference. As educators, therefore, it is an ethical necessity to free ourselves from totalizing signifiers and categories, a serious task toward which a praxis is proposed. I introduce here a way of semiotizing ourselves in the pedagogical encounter to help us wrestle with the sign before the signifier takes hold of experience, in order thus to instigate a freedom at the level of the *subpersonal*. Second, we must retrieve our affective investments from reified categories and decrystallize them so as to regain the power of becoming. Toward this I devote a section that discusses the Deleuze-Spinozist approach to active affect and transformation. Thus, it will be seen that, while the empirical part of the book is situated in a specific context, the conceptual work, in the scope of its experimental possibilities, takes it far beyond those limitations.

Early research had shown that the 'objective reality' of the formal organization called school is largely a result of the continual affirmation of rules, dispositions, and habits of thought through the everyday decision-making practices of teachers and administrators (Cicourel, 1963). In other words, it is through the boundaries and categories affirmed daily through organizational "habitus" that school is experienced in a certain way. The result is a structure of beliefs and categories that emerge as solid and stable in our signification systems, and depend on the habitual substratum of similarity and repetition for its perpetuation. Using a Deleuzian lens, I try to find ways of rethinking and experimenting with these signifying orders, that is, to relocate difference within repetition, in order to loosen them, that will allow us to move beyond those confining spaces, and release the positivity of difference. The two series—the empirical and the conceptual—will be interwoven to carry out this exercise.

In the case study, we see evidence of the limiting assumptions about the boundedness of the learning situation, the role of the teacher, and the fixed reference points of school subjects, all of which inhibit creative movement. The insecurity that I witnessed among new staff, when learning spills over in uncontrollable ways into the streets, off-campus placements, and beyond, and does not proceed in a linear fashion within a physical location, subject area, or measurable intervals, was the sense of loss of control.[6] But indeterminacy is not a lack, but a "perfectly objective structure" that acts as a fresh "horizon" within perception, as Deleuze (1994, 169) puts it.

The use of Deleuzian concepts is to help pry open reified boundaries that exist not just in thought, but as affective investments that secure those territorialities. The effort is to loosen them so that new modes of transformation become available that can enhance our affective capacities. The innovative program of the school held the promise of a different approach; in its effort to break away from more limiting approaches, it recognized that students learned things that are valuable to their becoming at off-campus locations, and in-between sites, in conversations between the sites, in the unbridgeable gaps between what they experienced and what language allowed them to express, and in gestures and modes of being that are often palpable but not measurable. But these possibilities were unevenly grasped, and teachers were often unsure how to hold the formations open, or, rather, how to prevent structures from closing in so as to let the various layers proliferate in intensities, and be able to multiply the connections between the curriculum, the ongoing rich experiences of the field, and the knowledge that their often difficult backgrounds offered. The result was the repetition of a structure of innovation rather than innovation itself. This is where a Deleuzian praxis, that talks of complex repetition, or difference within repetition, can help.

It is contended here that a more complex understanding on the part of the teachers of the nature of boundaries in which they are implicated and an attention to the resonance between divergent learning spaces and the discourses of beings in those spaces can open the door to a fruitful set of relationships that is both more fluid and generative. The Deleuzian notions I introduce help us to reopen petrified borders, as well as to look for the possibilities of gaps and fissures, and in-between spaces, where learning takes place in unusual and discontinuous ways. Or, to put it differently, the production of the space, or the opening of an irregular interval is not separate from the learning. Chapter 1 is devoted to the explication of some key Deleuzian concepts that frames the study, that pass into us as much as we pass into their oscillations and act as the primary tools of the investigation. In the present book, I try to be as economical as possible with Deleuze's vast *oeuvre*, introducing a concept only where and if absolutely necessary.

Deleuze is an "ethnographer" of the nomad; his philosophy tends to be injected with sudden microelements of lived experience drawn from history, art and literature that concretize the abstract formations, and is therefore valuable for the explication and theorizing of the case study. Through Deleuze, and the questioning of "dominant significations," we reach a plane of multiplicities, a "nomadic" terrain whose cartography is based on flight from "striated" or highly regulated spaces where life's endless flux is coerced into preexisting molds or "molar" formations. Escape from molarization involves *becoming "molecular,"* or entering microelemental passages of potential transformations, and resisting the overpowering forms of societal expressions that endlessly trap experience. In chapter 3, I investigate the in-between spaces in the school curriculum, the fissures, leakages, and slippages, that contain transformative possibilities, and that become visible when we use a Deleuzian map. I have said earlier that a key Deleuzian notion on which this book turns is that events and phenomena including identities are multiplicitous and constitutive of difference. Therefore, the search for praxis is a search for a way to operationalize this perception.

One way to enter this mode is to see the pedagogical encounter in terms of a system of signs. Signs arise when we encounter a difference or make a distinction; we navigate by means of signs, mapping out reality in terms of it. Through repetition of collective beliefs, predispositions, prevalent wisdom, power relations, and existential imperatives, groups of signs become isolated, and boundaries get drawn unifying them as this or that event (Deleuze, 1990a). This is a molarizing effect by which powerful forms of cultural expression are thrust on a group of signs unifying it into a category. For example, when curriculum developers and textbook manufacturers pounce on an idea, such as the notion of heuristics suggested by the mathematician George Polya (1957), and reify it into a curricular commodity, we see the emergence of a molar category.

But the limits placed around the sign, or rather, the process by which we construct the discreteness of an event or sign, often remain obscure to ourselves. Chapter 4 goes into the question of sign regimes and illustrates how, by means of semiotic experimentation—I call it an apprenticeship of the sign—these constructs may become more visible to us in the context of learning, helping us thereby to get away from stratified ground and onto a more open territory. Using a Deleuzian praxis to move away from dominant regimes of signification, I examine the micropolitics of the sign in the construction of the educational encounter, and simultaneously look at our own constitution by the sign. It is contended that by means of relentless experimentation we can escape being trapped in reified sign regimes and enter into new becomings and reintensifications.

The analysis also deals with the important issue of stress and affect in the teaching situation which is intimately tied to identity and curricular responses. Following Deleuze's work on Spinoza, chapter 5 examines how signs can be engaged so as to release our existential powers rather than diminishing them. It is to a pragmatics of the sign that I turn in order to theorize about the problem of teacher stress. That is to say, I shift the problem of affect from the domain of private experience to a semiotic space, and examine the images in thought that are the result of dominant significations. By this I hope to show that a certain manner of relation to signs and the concomitant image that we construct of ourselves has a certain relationship to the problem of stress.

The major operation in this book is, thus, the opening up of pedagogical boundaries as these arise out of the modes of being and thinking of the actors, in order to get beyond images that have become congealed in thought through habit. To get beyond these signifiers is to free the imagination. Such an operation is carried out by means of careful examination of, and experimentation with, sign regimes, as well as through the release of affective powers, by looking at the differential transforms and fluxes beneath our constituted selves. Deleuzian pragmatics allows us to envisage the production of new spaces for teacher perception and action, and to rethink educational commonplaces and thereby release us from the oppression of reified categories. It is my belief that such release brings with it a certain transformative energy, and a creative potential of difference, that has the possibility of releasing new powers of being and acting.

The concepts in terms of which I have been discussing the framework—signs, fields of flux, intensities, micro-intervals, affects, and so on—are characteristic of the descriptive mode of what one might call a posthumanist plane.[7] These descriptors, which can be identified in any part of the continuum of life and are not necessarily associated with the human, slide beneath our gross identities, in order to free thinking from the domination of fixed systems of signification through the instantiation of the singular and the production of difference. In the book, in general, my strategy for dealing with Deleuzian concepts has been to proceed not by defining them comprehensibly at the outset, but instead, allowing them to unfold by returning to them again and again in different contexts.

The Bigger Picture

More broadly, this book may be regarded as joining the stream of thought that James MacDonald and William Pinar have called a "reconceptualization" of the field of curriculum theory. Pinar (1994) states that the reconceptualization

> begins in fundamental critique of the field as it is. The order of critique distinguishes it from most reform efforts, efforts which accept the deep structure of educational and social life, and focus upon "improving it." The Reconceptualization aspires to critique which insists upon the transformation of extant structures. It must function to dissolve frozen structures. Thus implicit in such an analysis of contemporary educational practices is their transformation. (66)

Although Pinar (2002, 3) has subsequently referred to the contemporary scenario as "post-reconceptualist," I have used the term without the prefix to indicate the unending work of continuous transformation. Part of the work of reconceptualization involves looking at theory as experimental tools of thought in order to open up ideas about practice. Such labor attempts to transform the field of curriculum "into a theoretically potent, conceptually autonomous field which inquires systematically into the multi-dimensional reality that is education and schooling in ways that aspire to transform both" (Pinar, 1994, 71). And this infusing of the field with theory must be done, as Pinar has pointed out, in a manner that is sensitive and responsible to our present.

This book attempts to demonstrate that Deleuzian pragmatism can be appropriated and then reconstituted through educational experience to form an important conceptual matrix for advancing thinking in curriculum. It is especially relevant at this historical moment given the increasing tilt toward conservative agendas sweeping through most advanced capitalist societies and the consequent shrinking of public spaces, a tendency that Deleuze and Guattari (1987) have termed fascist-paranoid. Deleuze (1977) agrees with Foucault that theory "is a struggle against power, a struggle aimed at revealing and undermining power where it is most invisible and insidious." Deleuze adds that, "A theory is an instrument for multiplication and it also multiplies itself...and is by nature opposed to power" (208). In other words, theory, by inventing multiplicity, continually displaces and makes suspect all identitarian grounds that serve as foundations for the exercise of power. This is micro-resistance, or resistance at the minoritarian level. In bringing together the two series—the empirical data from the school and the Deleuzian constructs—the book attempts to generate an experimental space of "in-betweenness," an irregular dimension that can aid the task of rethinking aspects of curriculum by means of relentless experimentation on ourselves that open up our constituted selves to new becomings, which may be seen as a political process of reinscription. This book must not be seen simply as offering a new way of functioning in the urban environment, keeping intact implicit presuppositions about language, identity, and event. It challenges some rather fundamental assumptions about who we are as teachers and our relation to the sense-making processes that we must daily pass through and that must pass through us.

Notes

1. Relays are self-propagating impulses that have no particular material content but are transmissions by means of a potential difference.

2. In *A Thousand Plateaus*, Deleuze and Guattari explain: "Two sounds of equal pitch and different intensity cannot be compared to two sounds of equal intensity and different pitch. Multiplicities of this kind are not metric. They are anexact and yet rigorous" (483). In other words, these are neither exact nor inexact, but anexact, that is, lying beyond the metric dichotomy, in a nonmetric or non-Euclidean space.

3. Deleuze's urban orientation is contrasted to Heidegger, who was known as the "philosopher of the forest."

4. Image-copy is the Platonic notion of the "Idea" or ideal forms of which objects of experience are copies. Experience is thus subjugated and made to conform to a preexisting reality.

5. The dialectical method has a long history, and works through contradictions by juxtaposing opposites in order to arrive at a higher synthesis. It is a negative method that views difference and becoming as other than Being, which is supposedly fixed and eternal. In other words, all difference ultimately serves to bring us closer to Being. However, for Deleuze, difference is pure affirmation, it is life itself, and not a movement toward pure being or an ultimate truth. Deleuze therefore shuns the negative movement of the dialectic and its totalizing notion of an absolute ground. Other French poststructuralists such as Foucault have a similar position against the dialectic. As for pluralism, it is the refusal of any preexisting, unitary ground that organizes experience, affirming instead the plurality and the divergence of experience and therefore the possibility of new ways of being and becoming. It is a challenge to all forms of patriarchy which tell us how things ought to be.

6. Placements are service-learning centers where students are placed as part of their curricular requirements. This is explained at length in chapter 3.

7. Posthumanism does not recognize any clear boundary between the human and the nonhuman, and sees the "human" as a construction or assemblage of various other organic and nonorganic subsystems that Guattari calls "part-subjects," and that are found throughout the natural world.

Chapter 1

Curriculum and Representation

The problem no longer has to do with the distinction Essence-Appearance or Model-Copy. This distinction operates wholly within the world of representation. Rather, it has to do with undertaking the subversion of this world—the "twilight of the idols."　　　　　　　　　　—Gilles Deleuze, *The Logic of Sense*

Taking a Nietzschean view that it is necessary "*to learn to think differently*—in order to attain even more: *to feel differently*" (Nietzsche 1982, 103), Deleuze attempts, through what may be seen as a radical form of empiricism, to change the very image of thought that has dominated through the history of philosophy. And the image of thought challenged by Deleuze is representationalism: "According to this image, experience can be reduced to the interiority of a self-constituting subjectivity" (Hayden, 1998, 5). That is to say, representationalism assumes that thought is a faithful interior representation of the "outside" within an autonomous subject, and consequently, recognition becomes the chief tool of thought. This vastly affects pedagogy as it does other forms of experiences, as thought seeks and establishes unchanging forms, and laws, in the outside, upon which to found its activities. From Plato to Descartes, and Kant to Hegel, we find different forms of representationalism, and synthesis of the faculties occurring that affirms this view. One of Deleuze's key projects is to liberate thought from its representation-alist image that, according to him, has subjugated thought itself and inhibited it from functioning more freely. This is a position that Deleuze shares closely with Foucault.

And how does representation end up subduing thinking? In Deleuze's (1994) words,

> Representation fails to capture the affirmed world of difference. Representation has only a single centre, a unique and receding perspective, and in consequence a false depth. It mediates everything but mobilises and moves nothing. (55–56)

This model of thought subordinates the experience of difference to the notion of representation, seeking to validate experience from a "single center," and therefore leaves us "unable to think difference in itself" (Hayden, 1998, 6).

Immediately it is clear what it has to do with our problem. Representation captures the experience of difference and forces it to conform to the four criteria of representation, namely, identity, resemblance, analogy, and opposition (Deleuze, 1994), thereby suppressing difference itself in the interests of producing order and recognition.[1] The novice teachers I observed struggled to produce "similarity" in the midst of proliferating diversity, attempting to contain the abundance of difference within the Same. To liberate thought from the clutches of representation is to be able to think difference in itself and realize the productive power of difference. For it is difference rather than similarity—difference in temperature, density, currents, potentiality, for example—that drives all change and becoming in phenomena. Acknowledging this would allow the curriculum to expand in previously unthought-of ways, and make room for engaging constructively with uncertainty and contingence.

The inadequacy of traditional methods, which emphasized uniformity and manageriality (Blake et al., 1998) in the urban environment, was borne out in this case by the conversations I had with the founding teachers at the site of the empirical study who had opted out of the district curriculum in order to formulate their own, under an innovative program, and in whose assessment the mainstream approach did not serve urban youth well. In the language of the present analysis, the practices were overly determined by a representationalist mode of thought. I have theorized the above problem as it plays out in the specific instance of the case study as an issue of teachers carrying with them representationalist ways of constructing boundary distinctions around learning, teaching, identity, and processes of communication that mediated the complex reality that they faced in the urban setting. Apart from pedagogical consequences, there are serious affective ones including conflict, stress, and even burnout. While boundaries help us construct a reality out of the sensible, when reified they also cut us off from the subtleties of differential transformations that occur continuously in teaching and learning, as well as in experience in general. To put it in Deleuzian terms, pure repetition is impossible, and we must learn to look in the passages and transformations, at the outer edges of phenomena, for intimations of composite relationships and amalgamations.

In other words, the attempt here is to find ways in which to connect teachers to the positivity of difference. Such a praxis would allow teachers to draw on the productivity of difference and thus to connect more fruitfully and creatively to the divergent spaces of the urban environment. Instead of being passively affected by conditions, I look for ways in which teachers can affect the situation in which they find themselves by breaching or rupturing the old boundaries that can lead to a release of new intensities. This is the notion of "deterritorialization" in Deleuze—a movement by which we *leave the territory*, or move away from spaces regulated by dominant systems of signification that keep us confined within old patterns, in order to make new connections. For the very breach or rupture, when made with a certain conceptual preparation, or grasp of the "geology" of a new set of distinctions, becomes a production of differentiation that expands our powers of acting and affecting. Hence, an act of becoming (another important Deleuzian concept), rather than look for the similar, or the Platonic image-copy, seeks to *produce* difference, and thereby articulate new worlds.

To reiterate then, the site under discussion was a highly differentiated one in which the commonplaces of schooling had to be renegotiated again and again. The often unarticulated middle-class assumptions of schooling such as a stable home, a future orientation, the idea of continuity, and even average life expectancy could not be taken for granted. Students often talked of not living beyond thirty or thirty-five because they had not seen too many survive that age in their immediate surroundings. Middle-class becomings with their blessed-by-the-State trajectories and lines of development seemed somewhat alien on this landscape. The situation also demanded a curriculum that could take into account complex themes of uncertainty and loss, as articulated so well by Britzman (2002):

> Part of the loss we confront in the field of curriculum is the loss of our capacity to recognize our own psychical reality as being out of joint with ordinary reality. (96)

If we take the "psychical" to indicate a continually differentiating subjective reality with a kaleidoscopic mix of love, hate, fear, despair, and hope, then a curriculum directed mainly at "average," or a statistical reality, would appear to suppress the very ground in which learning could take root in differential spaces.

Given the pressure of internal differences that distinguish urban conditions from mainstream reliance on uniformity and homogeneity, teachers who come to appreciate difference, not to fetishize or hypostatize it, but to realize its creative potential, are more likely to succeed in positively contributing to the urban learning situation. And it is more than likely, as these pages will show, that they will also have a better chance of survival under these complex conditions if they allow conceptions to expand in ways other than confining learning to the limits of the repetitious outcomes that are mandated by the official curriculum. Citing Oliver and Gershman, Hartley (1997) observes,

> [E]ducation is supposedly about leading us away from where we are, but its effects may be to lock us into technical rationality as the only mode of thinking. In short, education ignores 'onto-logical knowing'…one which can include 'feelings, vague sensibilities, and inarticulable thoughts'…Here speaks the language of the unpredictable, of the imagination, of the passions …none of which are objectively reducible to discrete, analysable entities. (72)

Decades of Taylorism and Tylerism have narrowed and reified the bounds of practice (Kliebard, 1992), and it is mostly this 'other' of education that has been suppressed in the attempt to scientize learning and make education serve the interests of narrow goals. My attempt here is to help teachers find ways to allow these submerged sensibilities, murmurs, and unformed multiplicities to surface, by means of which we can explore new ways of thinking and feeling, and find ways of producing new and different effects in thought. The implicit belief is that such novel movements can help us to continually defer "stratification," or escape from existing structures of ossification.

The philosophy of Deleuze is eminently suited to the purpose of creating new terrain. Deleuze conceives of philosophy as a pragmatic practice of actively creating concepts that lead to new and different ways of affective thinking and being. He is the philosopher of difference par excellence, who has been referred to as "the difference engineer" (Pearson, 1997, 2), and whose effort has been to theorize difference by breaking away from representationalist ground:

> The primacy of identity, however conceived, defines the world of representation. But modern thought is born of the failure of representation, of the loss of identities, and of the discovery that …all identities are only simulated, produced as an optical effect by the more profound game of difference and repetition. We propose to think difference in itself independently of the forms of representation which reduce it to the Same, and the relation of different to different. (Deleuze, 1994, xix)

In the world of representation, "common sense," or the Kantian *concordia facultatum*, contributes to the form of the "Same." That is, at the heart of representation is the image of thought as subjective unity or a conjunctive synthesis of the faculties that produces correspondence. This powerful tradition has an overwhelming echo within the curriculum, which, operating within this image, aligns learning substantively with the notion of recognition. Hayden (1998) remarks,

> The representationalist image of thought portrays thinking not as the creation of new values and new senses, but as the proper allocation and distribution of established values and the verification of its own image. (27)

In other words, thought is confined to maintaining "correctness" of existing ideals, and to the allocation of established truth values rather than the creation of new ethical and sensory engagements. In this way, thought mirrors its own image in a process of internal reflection that largely shuts out new possibilities of perception-action. We want teachers to move away from this image of thought and create new values and new sense, and the poststructural discourse is an ally. Whereas, the modernist curriculum that dominates schools as well as most reform movements is really a redistribution and strengthening of existing structures. Hartley (1997) observes,

> And yet, whilst postmodern culture is centrifugal, curriculum Planners—despite the rhetoric of choice and diversity—withdraw to the centre, in a rearguard action, to re-group, not only themselves, but also the subjects of the curriculum, building in courses which will serve to integrate the fracturing self of the postmodern pupil. (73)

This attempt to integrate is a last ditch attempt to save representation, but cannot bring about new thinking in relations or provide solutions to the problem of difference.

What can Deleuze offer us here? Rejecting the representationalist image that what is encountered is experienced as recognition, Deleuze says, "Something in the world forces us to think. This something is an object not of recognition but of a fundamental *encounter*" (Deleuze, 1994, 139), and in whichever manner this something is grasped it can only be of the order of the sensible, and not of the order of recognition which presupposes the existence of categories of the possible. In rejecting recognition as the basis of thought, Deleuze is rejecting the application of the categories of the possible to real experience: "To apply the possible to the real as if it dictated what real experience can be is to posit a world of representation rather than to encounter the world of actual experiences" (Hayden, 1998, 29).

For Deleuze, the world is fundamentally heterogeneous, with perception the result of divergent series, that is, a consequence of disjunctive synthesis, and not convergence. Turning Platonism that sees the world as reproductions of an original Model on its head, Deleuze (1990b) posits the world as "simulacra," or copies without an original:

> To "reverse Platonism" means to make the simulacra rise and to affirm their rights among icons and copies. The simulacrum is

not a degraded copy. It harbors a positive power which denies *the original and the copy, the model and the reproduction.* (262)

To apply the possible to the real is essentialist thinking, whereby things proceed from ideal forms, or *eidos*, to the particulars, and experience must conform to essences. But for Deleuze, forms are not established prior to populations; instead, they are more akin to statistical processes that are abstracted from populations themselves. Therefore, we must give up thinking typologically, and instead, operate with the notion of multiplicities that continually diverge to produce ever new populations. Instead of approaching things as approximations of ideal states, we look for the advantages of variations; as there is no ideal image, we no longer seek degrees of perfection in terms of a type, but look in terms of differential relations, and coefficients of processes or intensive states. These primary processes, which I briefly discussed in the Introduction, are better grasped in terms of continuous variations of properties such as density, pressure, catalytic action, speed, mutation, and other variables. These differential relations drive all becoming, not categories.

But how do we connect these physical determinants to human actors in pedagogical settings? To grasp this, we must pause for a moment and turn our attention to the manner in which Deleuze views the human personality. Deleuze argues after Bergson that the human body itself is an image, empirically derived, that exists in reciprocal presupposition with other images in the world. That is to say, the body and the mind cannot but be images among other images, engaged in a complex and dynamic exchange, that create the sensation of being in the world. These images are *fundamentally elemental or impersonal,* and do not belong to the interiority of identity or personality. Instead, personalities or identities inhere in them, derived in a stochastic manner from these multiplicity of images.

Therefore, the personal, in Deleuze, "is understood as the empty site of passage between the subpersonal and the suprapersonal," that is, between the elemental and the notional (Massumi, 1992, 186). In other words, the person is not a thing in itself, but arises from moment to moment out of a certain movement between images or frames. Its organization depends on certain conditions which may change, producing entirely new effects in the so-called personality.

Once we are rid of all transcendental imagery, we can see the potentialities for change and becoming in terms of impersonal factors that are differential relations and molecular movements. By backing off from reified categories into the underlying fields of flux and variation, we shed layers of strata or *deterritorialize*, enabling ourselves to move from closed spaces into more open terrain. Here it is possible to reconsider our composites in terms of their constituent differences that are the key to the pragmatic possibilities that continually present themselves as pedagogical opportunities. How we do this is the subject of later chapters.

Also, and most important, growth, in Deleuzian spaces, does not occur by means of acquisition of systems, elements, or components, but by a loss: "It is through populations that one is formed, and through loss that one progresses and picks up speed" (Deleuze and Guattari, 1987, 48). That is, phase transitions take place through the loss of the characteristics of the previous plane. The emergent features are not acquisitions but differentiations. This provides us with an important insight into learning, which, in the modernist cast, is often pictured in terms of an acquisition model. In the Deleuzian diagram, elements of which we are beginning to draw out, learning becomes a production of difference, rather than acquisition. This is a much more helpful approach, especially with the disprivileged, whose narratives and ways of being are rarely taken seriously in the formal discourse of schooling.

But to be in contact with the arising of differential experiences in the senses, we have to renounce strong identification with categories. The powerful reasons for doing so will become clear by looking at the following examples from current issues in schooling. Let us for a moment consider the "whole language" versus "phonics" debate. Considered in Deleuzian terms, this is a phony debate, for it grows out of the hardening of the boundary lines around each of these categories, that is, by solidifying the strata by means of these very arguments. In other words, the battle lines are drawn through a *double articulation*—in turn, through a reification of categories, and then by making a pedagogic method out of these hardened distinctions, which further reifies, and so on. By the time we are well into this process, the two categories look distinct enough to be "real," and opposed to each other.

One way to resolve this dichotomy is through the method of textual deconstruction: by showing that phonics cannot be taught without a measure of whole language in which it is embedded, and that the so-called "whole language" must always involve certain reductionist moves from time to time. But Deleuzian pragmatics goes further than textual analysis. For Deleuze, text is only an extension of extra-textual practice. Deleuzian pragmatics contextualizes the problem by extracting from it the *singularities* of which the situation is composed.[2] The extraction of singularities would involve looking into the forces in the field that started the crystallization process, that is, the approaches to research, political alignments of authors, and materials that helped structure the debate in the first place, and by comparing it to narratives of actual situations of instruction to see how the idealizations get distributed in the field. A similar investigation could be carried out with the notion of whole language. In this manner, we create what may be called a vector field that shows the various series of diverging engagements that produce the singular. What is also important in such an analysis is that we ourselves are part of the field, and are not extrinsic to it. That is, we take into account our particular positioning within a milieu. The issue then no longer remains as a clash of clearly defined boundaries, but instead, a more fuzzy, fractal relationship emerges, wherein, when the attention shifts from the reified boundaries to the processes of their becoming, a wholly new composition becomes available.[3]

Consider yet another controversial topic such as religion in schools. There are those who vociferously oppose it as an infringement on religious freedom, and others who cannot imagine schools without religious instruction. Again, recasting the debate in Deleuzian terms, the issue takes on a completely different hue.[4] The debate produces what Deleuze would call "surplus value." That is, an excess generated by means of "interlocking syntheses" of incorporeal transformations induced by statements. These generate their own terms, gradients, and resonances, as they organize themselves through "infolding," or forming more stable relationships to neighboring enunciations or "judgments."[5] It is the surplus value or excess thus created that begins to determine the gradient of the terrain on which the debate carries on and hardens.

It is by recognizing that both sides have created a *surplus value* that merely strengthens their own respective terms of the debate, adding new intensities and forces as they roll along, without resolving anything, that we are alerted to the necessity of a different kind of investigation, in order that we may open up the boundaries and categories that reify like calcareous deposits at the edge of a pool. Teachers and students who undertake the careful and arduous task of mapping such a field would not only engage with the semiotics of religious instruction, as well as the assumptions of secular ideals, but also come to grips with the structurations of such discourses.

For Deleuze clarifies that all statements arise from *indirect discourse*, that is, from the multiplicitous murmurs, dialects, continuous variations, and nondiscursive presuppositions, all of which must be temporarily suppressed for the optical illusion of clear speech to arise. As Massumi (1992) has noted, "For a statement to appear in all its apparent simplicity and clarity, its complicated genesis must recede into the abyssal shadows from which it came" (46). In other words, every utterance is a Bakhtinian heterogeneity, but is morphed into a distinct enunciation by means of what Deleuze and Guattari call "order-words" (Deleuze and Guattari, 1987).

Order-words, a vital concept in Deleuze and Guattari's theory of language, do not constitute a particular type of statement; they are incorporeal transformations that make things fall into line with prevalent social norms and expectations. They are not a category, "but the relation of every word or every statement to implicit presuppositions" on which they stand (79). Order-words are not commands, but those that link statements to "social obligations." They produce redundancies by means of which statements and acts are connected, and by means of fixing the social gaze. For example, the statement "I swear" or the word "dating" gathers a certain force from the immanent social field through complicated sets of presuppositions and obligations that produce a certain act.

One insidious consequence of order-words is the plane of redundancy in which perceptions get immersed even as the rules of that reality game are already established by relations of power. A useful example is the projection of the notion called "school choice," whereby the order-word "choice" is projected as value-free and available for the asking. Thus, tacked onto a set of presuppositions the question is avoided as to who is really free to choose and under what circumstances. For Deleuze, language is neither information nor communication, but an endless transmission of order-words that leap from statement to statement or accomplish an act within a statement. Order-words can prove to be of great worth in analyzing the semiotics of institutions, especially of schools.

Concepts such as surplus value, order words, murmurs, the unsaid of every utterance, presuppositions, and the surface effect of enunciations slice open the grip of existing discourses and equip teachers and students with a set of new analytical tools with which to look at their social milieu as well as the codings and the boundaries within which they function. Moving beyond a critical approach, we are driven to the performative edge of those boundaries, and can experimentally observe how we are constituted at their conjunctions; we enter a praxis.

But to help us undertake such work, we also need to reexamine our relationship to signs, for according to Deleuze, what is encountered by the senses "is not a quality *but a sign*," that is, not something universal but differential, arising out of the clash of forces that produce a seething gradient of qualitative differences. Deleuze's approach to signs is more akin to Foucault's than to Saussurian systems. For Deleuze, an event or phenomenon is a sign, and the significance it has depends on the forces that occupy it at any time, thus constructing it out of the notion of continuous variation. If some signs appear stable, it is only because their current configurations are maintained or "overcoded" by strong forces, such as, for example, geologic ones. In the instance of schooling, the pedagogic encounter is an overcoding of the child, creating a supplementary dimension in which are inserted various transcendental and powerful unifying images of identity, conformity, nationalism, work, achievement, competition, success/failure, and many others. These overpower weaker forces of less unitary or chaotic activity.

Signs thus have the capacity to affect and be affected by other signs, and each sign refers not to an intrinsic state of things but to other signs in a chain of signification. Although the latter position is a poststructuralist one, Deleuze's approach to semiotics has elements in it that are not. For instance, Deleuze maintains that signs have content, but the content is not essence but an array of forces that occupy the sign at any given moment. And the sign perplexes us "as though the object of the encounter, the sign, were the bearer of a problem" (Deleuze, 1994, 140). In other words, each encounter or phenomenon posits a problem in the form of a sign that has to be engaged and experimented with. *Every* encounter is a fresh problematic, and invites a new struggle for meaning.

Using these Deleuzian insights that it is the differential as the sign that arises in an encounter rather than universals of representation, and that it is "the sensible multiplicities that are the conditions of actual experience" (Hayden, 1998, 35), I look at the learning encounters at the school in question, and find it exhibiting such slippages and leakages so as to constantly exceed and escape the representationalist space of technocratic rationality within which the signifying regimes of traditional curriculum tries to contain it. We see how events, pedagogy, curriculum, and relationships in the school are irreducibly multiplicitous rather than inhabiting the linearity or uniformity of techno-rational space, needing therefore mutant lines of thought that can engage productively on such a surface.

Therefore, I make the theoretical move of casting the problem of teacher becoming in semiotic terms, that is, as a problem of engaging and experimenting with sign regimes. I have argued in the book that novice teachers are better served by being educated to see the learning encounter as a system of signs they have to engage and experiment with, and not something they can take for granted or treat in terms of representation or recognition. Teachers have to *construct* the plane of divergence, the "planomenon," even as they encounter it, out of the differential experiences that are always in excess of what thought as recognition can expect.[6]

But this demands a very different mode of perception, and a manner of looking that cannot be from the static image of thought as representation, that is, from within the old habits of thinking. What can help us to disengage from deeply entrenched ways? For this we must realize the transcendental illusion that is involved in representational thinking. Representation assumes the possibility of pure repetition of an Idea, but this repetition is always in relation to a subject, and therefore *subject* to the differences of thought, affect, and consciousness within which it arises. This is made explicit here through an experimentation that leads to a semioticization of ourselves. To put it differently, we observe a relationship of *reciprocal presupposition* with signs. It leads to the understanding of the Deleuzian process of "disjunctive synthesis" through which matter-sign composites arise. This experiment is explained in detail in chapter 4.

The effort is to open ourselves up to signs in a manner that our composite natures that arise through reciprocal presupposition with signs become apparent. Experimentally rejecting the bondage to representation, we open a fissure into our molecular multiplicities in a lateral movement that challenges all hierarchical modes of thinking. In other words, we attempt, what Levi Strauss (1969) called, being situated at the level of the signs themselves, and Deleuze (1972) has called, being *immanent* to the sign. This is a *becoming* of the teacher unto the sign, a perception-action that changes the very image of ourselves from transcendent subjects existing outside the signs we perceive, to an immanent one in which we are no longer self presences looking at phenomena, but implicated in the signs themselves.

That is to say, the image of ourselves and reality is displaced from a universal and transcendental plane onto a *differential* and immanent one where we begin to act and move with the productivity of difference. It is only through a fundamental displacement of this nature, I argue, that a new approach to the problem of difference in pedagogic relations is possible. This results in a change in the very image of thought by initiating what Deleuze and Guattari (1983, 1987) call "schisis" or "secret lines of disorientation," as explained below.

With the invention of a new cartography wherein what was once regarded as a unified entity is redistributed semiotically over sign regimes, we find ourselves at the level of the sign. To proceed in this manner of deterritorializing, we make small ruptures in our everyday habits of thought and start minor dissident flows and not grand "signifying breaks," for grand gestures start their own totalizing movement, and are easily captured. Instead, small ruptures are often imperceptible, and allow flows that are not easily detected or captured by majoritarian discourses. This emphasis on the minor and the almost indiscernible is very important for the approach here.

These ruptures make connections across domains of signs through a *becoming* that displaces anthropocentric and humanist obsessions, allowing the emergence of multiplicities or matter-thought compositions that are always in the process of change, a becoming-other that creates new intensities and flows. For signs are hybrid entities, matter-thought conglomerates that have nothing inherently humanistic about them. The framework of the present discussion therefore is located on what may be thought of as a posthumanist plane that attempts to be free of points of unification as the basis of experience.

In *Anti-Oedipus*, Deleuze and Guattari (1983) offer such a framework which they call schizoanalysis. Schizoanalysis looks for *schisis*, or a break from dominant significations and usual patterns of thought that hold us captive by means of what William Blake had aptly called "mind-forg'd manacles." Its work is to disorient and displace us from the transcendent plane of the sovereign individual to one of composites and multiplicities, in which, instead of representation and resemblance, we have differential constructions and becomings. The dynamic constructivism of Deleuze comes out of the possibility of releasing the singularities trapped within our composites. The discovery of singularities or traits that have no name, label, or directionality allows us to glimpse the fields of flux and indefinitude that constitute us, as well as the events around us. The apprenticeship helps us to play an active role in such composition and thereby increase our affective capacities (Deleuze, 1972).

But we have to be careful here. I do not mean to celebrate or fetishize the notion of schisis or rupture for its own sake. Each schisis can lead to a new capture: For example, Capitalism is one such force of deterritorialization that constantly creates flux and uncertainty, and yet, at the same time produces new orders of enslavement. That is to say, the desires released through irruptive decoding of social mores, say, through technological innovation, are immediately captured in new crystallizations of consumption and social formations. Only a careful experimentation, knowing the risks, and finding or inventing new terrain in which the released forces could be distributed will make an endeavor such as this successful. An example is Guattari's (1995) clinical practice in psychiatry. Along with founder Jean Oury, Guattari worked the clinic La Borde as a collective enterprise where the usual distinctions between patient, doctor, and staff were mostly set aside in favor of overlapping and collective responsibilities. In this manner, "patients" were affirmed and became joint producers of the place, rather than passive receivers of treatment. Guattari thus fashioned a differential plane where deterritorialization found a creative escape. It also revolutionized the clinic. This example is particularly relevant here, since, as Foucault (1979) has shown, the clinic, the hospital, the prison, and the school have emerged from similar urges of disciplinary society.

A conceptual schema where difference is not a threat to an organizing principle, but of key productive potential, was vital to the task of arriving at a theory/praxis for a pluralistic enterprise at the school. The effort here is to realize by means of experimentation that difference is not an extrinsic phenomenon, but that we ourselves are the constructs of difference, multiplicities rather than identities. The study unfolds as a praxeological analysis that offers a way of looking at the learning encounter that helps teachers to emerge onto a new terrain of complexity and realize in the process the power of their own becoming and affective capacities.

One of my suggestions in this book is that in the midst of an unprecedented crisis of "civil society" (Hardt, 1998), and by extension, of liberal institutions therein, teachers and schools would be better served if they functioned with a differential cartography, rather than an identitarian one, and learn the new language of the mapping of intensities and becoming that leads to new possibilities. As to the relevance and necessity of engaging the elaborate theoretical machinery of Deleuze in considering the problem of teacher becoming, I contend that: First, as I have observed earlier, there is sometimes a necessity to change the very conceptual terrain on which we consider a problem, and I believe we are in that situation today with respect to teaching and schooling. The problem that I was encountering had much broader implications than the immediate context itself. The particular situation only served to highlight what is rather common in schools and other social institutions—the helplessness to appreciate and encounter difference without attempting to subject it to the identitarian pressures of dominant epistemologies (McCarthy and Dimitriadis, 2000a), that is, to the pressures of representation and recognition. Therefore, the issue deserved a deeper consideration and a level of theorizing that befitted its scope, since part of the task I have undertaken in the book is to go beyond the case study and develop an analytical framework for a different effort in curriculum.

A second, and equally important, point is that the existing approaches and frameworks have not resolved the problem that I address here, and instead, there is only increasing pressure on institutions to find ways of *managing* difference that keep things evermore the same, resulting in deep frustration for those on the margins. On this issue, teacher education programs have not done much more than include diversity as an added element to the existing discourse, an approach thoroughly, and rightly in my opinion, criticized by theorists such as McCarthy who observe that difference has been co-opted into the discourse of power "that attempts to manage the extraordinary tensions and contradictions...that have invaded social institutions, including the university and the school" (McCarthy and Dimitriadis, 2000b, 70). The thrust has been to "petrify" difference and absorb it into the mainstream instead of allowing it the more profound consideration that it deserves.

Finally, woven through the book is the productive and affirmative power of difference that is triggered through sidelining the old urge for representationalism, thus giving us the means to resist power and domination at the micropolitical or minoritarian level, something not found in psychoanalytic theory, social psychology, or the existing discourses on diversity and difference. For those interested in questions of freedom, divergence, power, and liberatory pedagogies, the present analysis provides important tools of thought as well as ways of becoming whose main thrust is to free spaces. Here, it will be helpful to relate the framework of the present study to some representational and non-representational perspectives. I will locate my position using rudiments of Marxism and Critical theory, some feminist positions, psychoanalytic theory, poststructural perspectives, and systems theory.

Deleuze and Marxism

Although both *Anti-Oedipus* and *A Thousand Plateaus*, two of the most well-known works of Deleuze (along with Guattari), are trenchant critiques of Capitalism and all forms of institutionalized domination and oppression that force our multiplicities into false totalities, Deleuze's approach to relations of production and power is different than those of the traditional left. First, I will run a single thread that is an intertext to many Marxist analyses in order to highlight this difference. By making a brief allusion to the theory of surplus value, which is basic to most Marxist positions, I will attempt to raise a useful distinction. Deleuze and Guattari (1987) observe:

> In these new [late Capitalist] conditions, it remains true that all labor involves surplus labor; *but surplus labor no longer requires labor.* Rather, it is as though human alienation through surplus

labor were replaced by a generalized "machinic enslavement," such that one may furnish surplus-value without doing any work (children, the retired, the unemployed, television-viewers, etc.). Not only does the user as such tend to become an employee, but capitalism operates less on a quantity of labor than on a complex qualitative process bringing into play modes of transportation, urban models, the media, the entertainment industries, ways of perceiving and feeling—every semiotic system. (492) (emphasis added)

The surprising insight that uncouples surplus value from labor, and shows it to be the result of complex qualitative processes that enslave through consumption rather than exploit through relations of production, is a powerful comment on cultural formations in late Capitalist societies. This can be a useful mode of analysis of the exploitative regimes let loose in schools through gross and subtle forms of commercialization (Molnar, 2002). Such an analysis goes beyond neo-Marxist ones in showing the mechanism through which children's bodies are opened up, with the connivance of the school system, for "vampiric extraction" of surplus value through consumption (Massumi, 1992, 81).

This is also a warrant for engaging a different plane of analysis whereby consumption, or the desire to be *passively* affected by other bodies, in a Deleuzian-Spinozist sense, can be resisted. Deleuze's work on Spinoza shows us the possibilities of transforming passive affects into active ones, that is, entering a plane where we learn to be producers rather than consumers of affect, thus reversing dependencies. This is very important from the point of view of the present analysis; it helps to create a new theoretical basis for resistance against the consumerist culture that reduces life and learning to the banal.

Therefore, it may not be inaccurate to say that although Critical theorists and neo-Marxists have criticized conspicuous consumption and Capitalism's culture industries, they have not fully come to terms with the fact that this has created a global space in which human destiny itself is recast (Deleuze and Guattari, 1987). In other words, Marxist positions fall short of giving us the tools necessary to escape subjugation on this emergent plane that requires new forms of resistance.

Second, Critical theorists "tend to employ a dialectical framework of analysis, and therefore, the analyses tend to explain relations in terms of opposing forces" (Fendler, 1999, 184). Arguments are cast within such traditional oppositions as oppressor/oppressed and empowered/subordinate. Deleuze's analysis, instead, follows nonbinary modes of differentiation such as "singularities," and change is seen in terms of becomings or formation of new multiplicities (Massumi, 1992). The trajectory of becomings of any composite cannot be known in advance, and therefore adherence to a priori categories becomes problematic. Also, Deleuze suggests that each constituted subject includes totalizing tendencies or micro lines of domination that need to be worked upon, and therefore there are no easy oppositions or platforms available. Careful selections have to be made from our multiplicities that have both de- as well as re-territorializing elements.

Instead of the broad class struggle of the Marxist lineage, Deleuze's political project and confrontation with power is mostly at the minoritarian level, concerned with the conditions of capture of the "molecular," or freer multiplicities, by the "molar," or forces of homogenization; that is, it looks at the conditions of possibility of specific struggles and resistances of different groups such as sexual minorities and other marginal social movements which Marxism treats as epiphenomenal to the historical antagonism between classes. Within the context of schooling, class analysis no doubt has brought to the fore several vital issues (see, for example, Bernstein, 1996, and Willis, 1977), but local and minoritarian movements are indispensable for preventing the strata or boundaries from locking us in. Deleuze and Guattari enter the micro-political dimension to look at the kaleidoscopic formations of desire and its becomings, and its potential in the struggle against hegemony. An awareness of the molecular within the molar, that is, the singularities within our constituted experience, create the possibilities of a "civil disobedience," to borrow a phrase from Rajchman (2000), that can direct our "badly analyzed composites" toward a constant *un*becoming, and therefore toward new social formations.

The phrase "badly analyzed composites," which Deleuze uses frequently to indicate the false unity of our molar identities, is again relevant from the point of view of students and schooling. It alerts us to the possibility of very different axes of analysis in our pedagogical encounters. For example, as Deleuze and Guattari love to point out, the binary X or Y may be replaced by X + Y +..., that is, the exclusive 'or' by the inclusive 'and.' The exclusionary 'or' is a movement of patriarchy, whereas the 'and' opens an escape route. Thus, it is not a question of Ebonics *or* Standard English, but *and*; the simple 'and' is one way of getting away from exclusionary logic.

While attention to the microdynamics of desire opens the door to the molecular politics of multiplicities, it is also a threat at the same time:

> There are so many dangers, and each line [of becoming] poses its own. The danger[s] of rigid segmentation or a break appears everywhere...The prudence required to guide this line, the precautions needed to soften, suspend, divert or undermine it, all point to a long process of labor directed not only against the State but against itself as well. (Deleuze and Guattari, 1983, 95–96)

Thus, unlike Marxism, which discounts individual struggle, Deleuze warns that we not only must struggle against the state but against ourselves as well. Further, Deleuze and Guattari caution us of "micro-fascisms that exist in a social field without necessarily being centralized in a particular state apparatus" (97). In other words, all struggles themselves contain the potential of becoming new hegemonies. All this points to a level of complexity in Deleuzian ethics and dynamics of struggle and a differential politics of thought not usually found in Marxist analyses.

Finally, as I have mentioned earlier, Deleuze detects a kind of violence that remains outside the state apparatus not conceived of by Marxist analysis. Rajchman (2000) notes that it appears as

> a violence of forces that no state can control or rationalize in advance, and which comes to the fore in cities or is worked out through city rather than state-forms....Indeed one might say that in Deleuze, a city-state tension tends to replace the great state-society distinction that Foucault came to see as the chief limita-tion of modern political thought. (103)

This uncontained element is a force of "deterritorialization" that eludes capture and regularization by the State. It is a violence that always hovers at the fringes of order and upsets the totalizing calculations of power. Deleuze's subtle theorization of the city in terms of a certain quality of molecular violence that is not fully captured by the State machinery evokes powerful subversive energies and intertexts, and reverses the usually dismal picture of urbanity. This must not be mistaken as the adoption of a romantic attitude to urban violence and decrepitude; in fact, the violence must not be confused with the street type of aggression, but a tendency toward molecularization[7] that state apparatuses dislike because it is a violence in thought that makes us less predictable, and for Deleuze a new thought is born of a violence in thought.

Feminisms and Deleuze

Next, we will look at Deleuze's approach vis-à-vis some feminist positions, broaching it with a quote from Elizabeth Grosz, an anti-essentialist feminist writer whose work on Deleuze is widely cited. Grosz (1994a) observes that Deleuze and Guattari's

> notion of the body as a discontinuous, non-totalizable series of processes, organs, flows, energies, incorporeal events, speeds and durations, may be of great value to feminists attempting to reconceive bodies outside the binary oppositions [of] mind/ body, nature/culture, subject/object and interior/exterior oppositions. They provide an altogether different way of under-standing the body in its connections with other bodies. (164–65)

Grosz sees Deleuzian conceptions of the body and the Spinozist refusal to subordinate the body to the mind as a possible way of undermining the phallocentric positioning of the female body. Deleuze (1988a) has argued that the body always exceeds the consciousness we have of it, and therefore we do not know what the body is. In Grosz' work there is a sense that Deleuze's writing contains resources that can help feminists map bodily practices that evade the masculinist notions of the self.

There are others (Shukin, 2000; Irigaray, 1985), however, who warn against hasty adoption of Deleuze's texts in feminist thought. While they agree with Grosz about its potential for escaping Platonic thinking, at the same time, they also feel that Deleuze's works mythicize and fetishize the feminine without paying attention to the actual conditions of embodied women. Shukin (2000) writes on an apprehensive note,

> Throughout *A Thousand Plateaus*, Deleuze and Guattari indirectly summon up philosophical and social texts with foreboding investments. Deleuze believes, perhaps, that his own iconoclasm is enough to redirect the force of these allusions to subliminally power his own purposes....I would suggest, however, that while Deleuze does manage to siphon enormous affective energy off intertexts that are evoked without being raised, an inexorable weight of allusions pressures his thinking into old molds— particularly when it comes to sexual difference. (152–53)

The allusions to the limitless possibilities of geography in Deleuze's writings evoke in some feminist minds "colonial anticipations" and male adventurism. The frequent references to woman-becomings as a "path to original potency" summon up existing "exploitative discourses of animalisation and sexualisation" of the feminine in the popular media. In other words, the objection is that, while Deleuze points to new possibilities for women, in his writings, gender remains latent and women "a sort of threshold or medium" for possibilities rather than "embroiled" actualities (Shukin, 2000, 153–54). But animalization, it is important to realize, has little to do with *animal-becoming*, with which Deleuze is concerned. The former is part of an insidious chain of Oedipalized discourses, whereas the latter is the reconfiguration of stratified, molar identities into nuanced domains.

Also, to Shukin's question above as to whether Deleuze and Guattari can "control" the involuntary allusions to exploitative intertexts in their work, one must respond that Deleuze and Guattari's strategy seems to be to take the potency and the potential released by evocative and powerful intertextual material so far forward as to subvert their own processes; that is, to a point where they cannot recover their original ground in the reader. Massumi (1992) observes:

> The feminine gender stereotype involves greater indeterminacy (fickle) and movement (flighty) and has been burdened by the patriarchal tradition with a disproportionate load of paradox (virgin/whore, mother/lover). Since supermolecularity involves

a capacity to superpose states that are "normally" mutually exclusive, Deleuze and Guattari hold that the feminine cliché offers a better departure point than masculinity for a rebecoming supermolecular of the personified individual....Becoming-woman involves carrying the indeterminacy, movement, and paradox of the female stereotype past the point where it is recuperable by the socius as it presently functions. (87)

Therefore, bodies of either sex are urged toward a becoming-woman which takes us beyond the limit of recuperability of gendered individuality.

Along a different trajectory, feminists such as Alice Jardine (1985) have objected to the tendency in Deleuze's writings to ignore macropolitical and macrohistorical struggles in favor of minoritarian ones. Jardine also objects to the dispersal of identity in Deleuze's work, and the active encouragement to *become* other, that is, to be indiscernible or faceless. To this it is possible to argue that for Deleuze and Guattari, macropolitical struggles that are waged in terms of well-recognized patterns of signification cannot get to the micropolitics of desire at the level where many of the struggles are actually located. Deleuze's effort is to create a geography of intensities that is free of all ideal significations and Platonic taint that have enslaved thought and maintained territories of exploitation.

In Platonism and all patriarchal systems, Deleuze and feminists have a common enemy. In order to appreciate the significance of Deleuzian resistance, we have to understand that struggles against domination and against patriarchal systems are carried out not only in groups and collectivities, but also within the micro-multiplicities of subjects in uncontrolled, secret, and subterranean ways. Thus, there are "nonrepresentative struggles, struggles without leaders, without hierarchical organizations, without a clear-cut program or blue-print for social change, without definitive goals and ends" (Grosz, 1994a, 193). That is to say, while overt struggles with recognizable ends, leaders, symbols, and means are important, faceless struggles that have no particular definition must and do occur alongside, every moment. It is mostly to this kind of struggle to escape patriarchy and domination that Deleuze and Guattari address themselves:

It is, of course, indispensable for women to conduct a molar politics, with a view to winning back their own organism, their own history, their own subjectivity....But it is dangerous to confine oneself to such a subject which does not function without drying up....It is thus necessary to conceive of a molecular women's politics that slips into molar confrontations. (Deleuze and Guattari, 276)

Molar or majoritarian political projects tend to dry up without corresponding struggles at molecular or minoritarian levels. It is a misunderstanding to think that Deleuze is privileging the individual struggle over the collective. For Deleuze, the so-called "individual" is always already a collective, a multiplicity, and therefore molecular confrontations must not be understood as individualistic and solitary escapades but new movements of desire unhindered by modernist images of the self. Foucault (1983) has noted that the question raised by Deleuze is: "How can and must desire deploy its forces within the political domain and grow more intense in the process of overturning the established order?" (xii).

These struggles without faciality need different tools and conceptions such as schizoanalysis that can de-Oedipalize our subjectivities and release affective energies for new forms of resistance. It is the theorizing of these faceless, subterranean struggles that makes the Deleuzian approach so valuable and relevant for looking at curriculum and teacher becoming. While category-based struggles are valuable, teachers must carry resistance into the micro-spaces of difference and reconstitution, that is, into a caring for the self (Swaminathan, forthcoming) that makes the possibility of change at the grassroots level more conceivable.

Deleuze and Psychoanalysis

Let us also, briefly, locate Deleuze with respect to yet another major twentieth century discourse—Freudian psychoanalysis. In Western metaphysics, from Plato to Lacan, desire has been seen as a lack in being that strives to be filled through the impossible attainment of an object. Deleuze comprehensively rejects this position. Like some feminists, Deleuze (1995) attacks the totalization of desire in Freudian psychoanalysis, refuting the basic Freudian position of the unconscious as the Oedipal theater: "We attack psychoanalysis on the following points which relate to its practice as well as its theory: its cult of Oedipus, the way it reduces everything to the libido and domestic investments..." (20). For Deleuze, the libido is invested in the social field in complex ways that cannot be captured within the reductionist space of the Oedipal structure. His attempt is to release the so-called libido, which itself is an order-word, from the grip of this structure. In Foucault's (1983) view, Deleuze and Guattari combat "the poor technicians of desire...who would subjugate the multiplicity of desire to the twofold law of structure and lack" (xiii). This highly limited view, one that has had a powerful impact on twentieth-century thought, has prevented the conceptualizing of desire in other ways.

First, let us look at the question of the unconscious and make a distinction between the two positions. For Deleuze, the unconscious is not a repository of submerged feelings or a product of repression, nor is it a dialectic between the Imaginary and the Symbolic as in the Lacanian model. Giving a telescopic view, Massumi (1992) writes that in the Deleuzian conception,

> the unconscious is everything that is left behind in a contraction of selection or sensation that moves from one level of organiza-tion to another: It is the structurations and selections of nature as contracted into human DNA. It is the multitude of excitations of rods and cones and nerve cells as contracted into a perception of the human body. It is the perceptions of the human body as contracted into larval selves. (83)

In other words, fashioned out of the overflows, leftovers, and latencies of successive levels of actualization, the unconscious is in a continuous state of production, as the aggregate, that is, of the human body's moves between states. It is ceaselessly in motion, and hence continually changing in architecture. There is nothing particularly humanistic about this interlocking synthesis of various levels of subpersonal becomings.

Similarly, for Deleuze, desire "is never a strictly personal affair, but a tension between sub- and superpersonal tendencies that intersect in the person as empty category" (Massumi, 1992, 82). In other words, the person is the product of the endless play of desire and arises at an intersection of specific interplays. Deleuze rejects the Freudian position that desire is desire for an object, whether phallus or breast.

Following Spinoza and Nietzsche, Deleuze turns desire around and understands it as *primary, positive, and productive*. Instead of aligning desire with fantasy and illusion, as psychoanalysis does, Deleuze sees desire as what *produces* the real, creating connections, relations, and alignments. For Deleuze, desire is a relation of effectuation, not of satisfaction; it is the primary producer of reality and all relations within it. In Foucault's (1983) words, Deleuze and Guattari attempt to free us from the "old categories of the Negative" (xiii). It is possible to add that this dramatic inversion of Freudianism must have positive theoretical consequences for feminist positions as well, since women have traditionally been framed as the repositories of that lack within male epistemologies.

To free ourselves from the reductive psychoanalytic and Oedipal yoke is to take a step toward freeing the multiplicity of desire from bondage to totalities. But the problem of desire remains, and since we can no longer leave desire in the hands of the experts and professionals, who are seen by Deleuze and Guattari as agents of the state, we have to analyze and actively engage in ethical experimentation in order to make new "connections" in the production of the real; through a proliferation of connectivities, there is the possibility that we might escape Oedipalized territory.

This is significant from the point of view of learning, teacher development, and curriculum. For by radicalizing the conception of desire as irreducibly multiplicitous and affirming it as the very site of production, we take a step toward constructing a curriculum of intensities, leaving the ground of boundaries and categories. An example might be worthwhile here:

I am in a mathematics classroom. The teacher is at the board explaining linear equations and coefficients. At the rear are two boys executing some exquisite steps in an intricate dance sequence. They are noticed eventually and are evicted, no doubt to be followed by other inevitable consequences. (Excerpt from Case Journal)

The acting out with bodies complex rhythms that did not find representational expression on the board was instantly condemned, the Oedipal structure swooping down on them, curbing the expression of desire.

While I am hardly suggesting that breaking into dance in the classroom is an adequate response to mathematics, the semiotization of those expressions could contribute much to the learning of math, showing the two apparently irreconcilable series—the chain of mathematical signification (see Walkerdine, 1988) and the expressions of intensity—as not necessarily antagonistic. Instead, a very different set of Oedipal lines were drawn whose ultimate consequence could only be the turning of desire against itself. In line with Deleuze and Guattari, who use the term 'Oedipal' to allude to different forms of "statization" or the confinement of experience within officially sanctioned striated space, I will use the term in this broader sense.

Deleuze and the Poststructuralists

Next, we will place Deleuze against what goes by the name of poststructuralist discourse. I will begin by comparing Deleuze to Foucault; the two thinkers often appear very close in their utterances and political commitments. Although treated as poststructuralists, Deleuze as well as Foucault can be distinguished from other writers of that genre. In *Truth and Power*, Foucault (1984) observes, "I believe one's point of reference should not be to the great model of language (*langue*), but to that of war and battle. The history which bears and determines us has the form of a war rather than that of a language: relations of power, not relations of meaning" (56). With this Deleuze would agree wholeheartedly. In fact, in Deleuze and Guattari's (1986) monograph titled *Nomadology: The War Machine*, as well as scattered throughout their other works, are references to this different point of reference, of a machinery of war that is key to understanding social formations and the clash of forces.

But a different distinction between Foucault and Deleuze may be useful here, not in order to oppose them, for there is a great deal of resonance between the ideas of the two, but to bring out the subtle differences so that they can better complement each other. While Foucault talks of power, Deleuze talks of force. Both Foucault's 'power' and Deleuze's 'force' are constitutive and productive. But "Force is not to be confused with power," says Brian Massumi, one of the most insightful readers of Deleuze, "power is the domestication of force. Force arrives from outside to break constraints and open new vistas" (foreword in Deleuze and Guattari, 1987, xiii). One way to understand Deleuze's notion of force is to consider the discursive and the nondiscursive and what brings them together in social action. Massumi (1992) gives the example of a set of instructions for woodworking which gets translated into certain actions on the wood although

> the interrelation of relations between the wood and the tool bears no resemblance to that between concepts, which bears no relation to that between phonemes or letters. (17)

The implication here is that there is an abyss between the discursive and the nondiscursive, or the visible and the articulable, that is bridged by force, a specific and contingent configuration of which has also called a "diagram" by Deleuze. Without force that is always already present, the worker, the instructions for woodworking, the tools, and the wood could not come together. Force then also acts like insight, which makes the connections. Further, according to Massumi (1992), what makes any action repeatable, what multiplies it, is a regularizing network of forces. "And since the action of this reproductive network of forces is qualitatively different from that of the productive network of forces from which the event arose" in the first place, we must make a distinction. We give the reproductive network another name— "power," in order to distinguish it from force (19). Therefore, while power is the relations of regularization, force is the instance and the bridging moment between the discursive and the nondiscursive.

Second, in *The History of Sexuality*, Foucault writes:

> It is over life, throughout its unfolding, that power establishes its domination; death is power's limit, the moment that escapes it; death becomes the most secret aspect of existence, the most "private." (Foucault, 1984, 261)

The notion of power, then, in Foucault is seen to be closely aligned with the unfolding of the human condition. Death is "power's limit," that is, in death there lies the possibility of a final escape from power or repetition. Power is thus constitutive mainly of social existence and relations.

It is precisely this human, organicist aspect that is absent in Deleuze's notion of power or force. For Deleuze, the "immanent life that is pure power" is "impersonal and nonorganic...that goes beyond any lived experience" (Deleuze 1997, xiv). It is, instead, "an ontological concept" in which virtual qualities become actualized in determinate space-times. Deleuze's reading moves the concept of force toward the impersonal, toward an "outside." Although, at first glance, this might seem somewhat essentialist, Deleuze is clear that force is always contingent and ever becoming without an *arche* or a telos, to borrow a famous Derridean phrase.

In *Cinema 1: The Movement-Image*, Deleuze (1985) shows how Vertov attempts to attain, through cinematic means, a vision released from human coordinates, a prehuman perception in a "any-space-whatever" (40). Similarly, Deleuze (1997) speaks appreciatively of Cézanne's ideas wherein form or even matter give way to forces, densities, and intensities: the tectonic folds in a mountain, the forces of germination in an apple, to what Cézanne referred to as the "dawn of ourselves" or "iridescent chaos" from which the stubborn geometries of our world later emerge (xxxv). Here, death is not "power's limit"; instead, death itself is a reordering of connections, of making momentarily visible the ordinarily invisible.

Finally, while Foucault talks of "limit experiences" that generate new forms of subjectivity, Deleuze's intervention takes a metaphysical turn in which "concepts" are created and "ontological speculation prepares the terrain for a constitutive practice" (Hardt 1993, 105). So, while Foucault's pragmatics operates through a negation, "through a refusal" of the kind of subjectivity that "has been imposed on us for centuries" (Foucault, 1984, 22), Deleuzian pragmatics operates through an ontological construction and experimentation with concept formation. I see the two as bearing in on the same project but from two different planes, with different coordinate systems, and with important differences in methods and tools. For Deleuze, "when words and things are opened up by the environment without ever coinciding, there is a liberation of forces which come from the outside" (Deleuze, 1988b, 87). It is this emphasis on "force" as also something operating on a space of the "Outside" that distinguishes Deleuze's force from Foucault's power, while at the same time, the very notion of the Outside Deleuze borrows from Foucault.

From the point of view of the case study, the establishment of a posthumanist ground using the notion of force is useful. For in the construction of a terrain of multiplicities, or the "rhizome" (Deleuze and Guattari, 1987, 3), what is important is to get rid of anthropocentric obsessions and humanist images before we can even begin to imagine ourselves as collectivities put together by an aleatory Outside. So, although teacher becoming, which is our central issue here, may appear to be something personal, it is really a matter of getting away from personalist conceptions toward a more tectonic and geographical distribution of forces and intensities through which one can be a producer of affective power.

Again, situating Deleuze relationally to Jacques Derrida may be useful here. Although both Derrida and Deleuze are staunchly anti-Hegelian, their attack on the totalization in the dialectic takes different paths. Referring to Derridean deconstruction, Deleuze (1997) writes:

> As for the method of deconstruction of texts, I see clearly what it is, I admire it a lot, but it has nothing to do with my own method. I do not present myself as a commentator on texts. For me, a text is only a small cog in an extra-textual practice. It is not a question of commentating on the text by a method of deconstruction, or by a method of textual practice, or by other methods; it is a question of seeing what *use* it has in the extra-textual practice that prolongs the text. (xv-xvi)

Thus, while for Derrida there is "nothing outside of the text" or "there is no outside text," or "there is nothing that is not a text," as his famous line *il n'ya pas de hors lexte* has been variously translated, for Deleuze it is the *extratextual* practice that "prolongs the text" that is of primary concern. Using Luhmann's (1990) insight that the world emerges at the same time as our description of it, the text can be said to emerge simultaneously with extratextual practice. Looked at in this manner, there is always an emergent "Outside" of the text that remains cognitively unapproachable to it, except a posteriori. Thus, Rajchman (1998) notes that Deleuze "makes construction the secret of empiricism," and that "deconstruction is not a word in his idiom" (2–3).

In other words, close textual analysis that exposes inherent contradictions in the text is not Deleuze's style. Instead, he appropriates selectively from the texts that serve his pragmatic purpose. That is, although Deleuze, in an apparently similar fashion to Derrida, seizes hold of the works of previous philosophers such as Spinoza, Nietzsche, and Bergson, unlike Derrida his work is not directed toward a deconstructive reading of those works. Instead, Deleuze is after ethical praxis, and describes himself as a "constructivist." Reading selectively, with Bergson, Deleuze develops an ontology; with Nietzsche, he sets that ontology in motion to constitute an ethics; and with Spinoza he takes a further step in this evolution, toward politics. His method is a process of accumulation and constitution. Ontology inheres in ethics, which in turn inheres in politics.

Deleuze's relationship with an "Outside" also allows him to deal with the danger of idealism, something that threatens much of the poststructural oeuvre. Critics such as Taussig (1993) and Massumi (1995) have noted that one of the central ironies of postmodern theoretical discourse is that the social constructionist critique of transcendence (i.e., reference to an independent reality) and the metaphysics of presence (i.e., inherent authorial meaning), that was meant to return meaning and interpretation to the social, historical, institutional and material processes of their production, has turned instead into its own form of idealism. By making human language the measure of all things, these critics allege, the poststructural oeuvre is threatened with linguistic idealism.

How does Deleuze's work meet this challenge? I will quote Boundas (Deleuze, 1993) on this question:

> Deleuze's thought cannot be contained within the problematics of the now fashionable textual allegory. The main thrust of his theoretical intervention is in the articulation of a theory of transformation and change or, as he likes to say, of a theory of *pure becoming* that, together with a language adequate to it, would be sufficiently strong to resist all identitarian pressures. It is this relentless effort to articulate a theory of transformation and change...that motivates Deleuze to replace Being with difference, and linear time with a difference-making repetition. (4)

This intervention in the form of transformation escapes the over-determination by the linguistic sign by breaching the known in the process of becoming. The world arises at the same time as the cognitive being, and therefore is not available as a text in the instant of becoming. There is a relationship with the "Outside" of thought that can be better understood from the systems perspective.

Deleuze and Systems Theory

Like Nietzsche (1967), who believed that the task of philosophy is to create possibilities and modes of existence, Deleuze and Guattari are incessant concept creators with which they forge new relations, bringing into view new distinctions. Discussing the work of concept creation, Deleuze and Guattari (1994) make the observation that no concept is ever complete, for that would be tantamount to invoking primordial chaos, that is, in which there is no distinction. Every concept is therefore limited and "irregular," and is "a matter of articulation, of cutting and cross-cutting" (15-16). And further, they continue, "The concept is defined by its consistency, its endoconsistency and exoconsistency, but it has no *reference*; it is self-referential; it posits itself and its object at the same time as it is created" (22).

The idea that concepts are a matter of "cutting and cross-cutting," and that they are "self-referential," resonates strongly with certain key notions of systems theory and especially the work of Niklas Luhmann (1990). Luhmann writes that all observation is incomplete and generates paradox and blind spots:

> The source of a distinction's guaranteeing of reality lies in its own operative unity. It is, however, precisely as this unity that the distinction cannot be observed....Another way of expressing this is to say the operation emerges simultaneously with the world which as a result remains cognitively unapproachable to the operation. (76)

The Deleuzian notion of concept can thus be seen as a close parallel to Luhmann's notion of distinction. Just as the viability of a Deleuzian concept is based on its consistency, the guarantor of the reality of an observation or distinction in Luhmann's case is its own "operative unity." In other words, both are self-referential. This is highly significant from the point of view of curriculum, for if the world arises simultaneously with the concept or distinction that we make, then it is clear that the effort toward pure repetition or *eidos* is falsely conceived, and that it keeps curriculum, students, and teachers mired in ungenerative pursuits, resulting in frustration and violence, especially among underprivileged groups who have no stakes in preserving the illusion of repetition, or maintaining the existing order. In other words, the challenge is to move from decoding life within an existing schema to producing those existential moments themselves.

The second important point of similarity is between Luhmann's notion of "world" or "environment," and Deleuze's (1988b) concept of the "Outside." Their respective analyses lean on a similar distinction—system/environment and concept/outside, but these are never absolute dualities, for what is system in one context can appear as environment in another. For both, the environment and the Outside, are inexhaustible, but with an important difference. In Deleuze's work, the inexhaustibility tends to appear as a positivity, that is, as a field of potentialities or virtualities, whereas for Luhmann, the inexhaustibility arises out of the possibility of new observation or new distinctions. For Deleuze, these potentialities or virtualities "exist" in terms of "unformed matters or intensities" (Deleuze and Guattari, 1987, 511), as latencies like that of the quantum world (Murphy, 1998) that can be actualized or drawn into zones of proximity by means of making connections, in order to produce infinite unique expressions. For Luhmann, new worlds can be brought into existence by making a new cut or observation.

Such views are liberating, to say the least, and contrast sharply with efforts to standardize curriculum and assessment, and other measures that produce inflexibility in the system. New "cuts" or observations have the potency to bring forth new worlds and are our escape from the status quo. For in a Deleuzian schema, it is only the construction and proliferation of connections that can be considered "real."

Deleuze's work also has close points of correspondence with the work of the systems theorists Humberto Maturana and Francisco Varela. Maturana and Varela's (1998) notion of "structural coupling" between system and environment resonates with the notion of becoming in Deleuze:

In an organism…[the] realms of interaction open the way to *new phenomena* by allowing new dimensions of structural coupling. (176) (italics in original)

For Maturana and Varela, the world is not a given, but is brought forth continually through the very act of living or structural coupling. Their term for self-referentiality is "autopoiesis," or self-generation that brings forth a world, and in the very process of world creation a new cognitive being emerges every moment.

Further, Varela (1992) talks of microidentities and microworlds that are the result of continual transition of the living organism from one state of readiness-for-action to the next. In Deleuze, we see its resonance in "nonformal functions" that find expression on a plane of continuous variation (Deleuze and Guattari, 1987, 511).[8] There are no stable entities, only dynamic states—singularities—that combine and recombine and are drawn into temporary *assemblages*. It points to a world populated by structures that are accretions of a complex mixture of geological, chemical, sociobiological, and linguistic constructions shaped and hardened over time. These accretions at each point set up the matrix for further accretions, and their biological, social, or mathematical components are inextricably mixed to produce temporary coalescences or microidentities, or matter-thought multiplicities or singularities—terms used more or less interchangeably here.

In pedagogic terms, this means that any encounter, say, between teacher and student, is a situation where multiplicities encounter other multiplicities and not identities. As will be explained later, these are not numerical multiplicities, but qualitative ones, variations of intensities on a continuous plane. When identities meet, there is the dialectic, with opposing positions and so on, bringing with it existent structures and teleological notions. Difference under such conceptions is only a means to a synthesis, and must ultimately be subsumed. But when multiplicities meet there is a porosity; there are openings through which new connections and synergistic combinations can be made. Difference here is affirmation and not negation. When, for example, as a teacher we face the intensity of a student's hostility, we might, instead of shrinking from it or opposing that state, or heaping upon it conciliatory gestures, draw upon that very differential affect without threatening to annihilate it with carrot or stick. That is to say, we encounter it as a field and not as a determinate incarnation.

But this requires a certain kind of work, a fashioning of the self after Foucault (1988), as well as a willingness to move away from the comfort of established or territorialized pathways and reconceptualizing oneself. Working through the above concepts, together with a willingness to experiment with novel existential moments, we may become open to what Deleuze, in line with Foucault, calls the thought from the "Outside." The Outside is the dangerous line that shows itself whenever we live sufficiently intensely; it carries us into "breathless regions." Breathless regions are regions of pure becoming that are literally breathless because of an altered relationship between the layers of determination. There is nothing mystical about this; one has only got to consider the fetus in a state of becoming, for instance, as a rough approximation. But our work is not to be carried off by this "deadly" line that in a sense is really a pure confrontation between the actual and the virtual, between life and death, "but to make [this line] endurable, workable, thinkable" (Deleuze, 1995, 111). This line is deadly because there is no real distinction here between the organic and the nonorganic, between one becoming and the next; it is impersonal like lightning. In other words, we have to remain in continual and careful relationship with this line of intensity and creative uncertainty, and make it work for us productively.

It could be said that this is, in a vital sense, the work of the educator: to find ways of staying on this line and continually push against stratification, and survive "while still confronting" it. This confrontation yields the necessary energy to deal with the everyday without reducing it to the mundane, and is helpful for constructing a plane of pedagogic relations, especially in working with marginalized youth—nonmainstream people who have sources of experience that are usually ignored or disvalued—and entering into a composite plane of becoming. This confrontation displaces us from our molar certainties.

The reference to microidentities above shows the usefulness of Maturana and Varela's work in clarifying the Deleuzian position, and I rely on it at several junctures in order to draw analogies. The notion of producing or "bringing forth a world" reveals a deep ethical responsibility in each existential moment, which is coplanar with Deleuze's notion of multiplicity and the necessity of producing difference so as not to be enslaved by dominant patterns, and the worn-out spaces they occupy. Further, the inexhaustibility of an Outside or the open link with the environment is also an indicator that reality or the system is not a given, and we can collectively change it.

So far we have been discussing the conceptual framework of the study, with a view to developing some basic Deleuzian concepts that might allow us to map a more open and generative approach to teacher education and curriculum but with reference to the constraints and the specificity of practice. And it is practice that we will meet next by moving to the site of the empirical study, to teachers and the school context involved in my observations. I will devote the following chapter to providing a certain amount of background on the case that will help situate our discussion. But I must add that what follows is by no means a "thick description" of the case, but simply an outline of the context. It allows us to view the basic workings of the school and the pedagogical structure within it, as well as the problems of practice that are of interest here. The experience of the site will be used to draw out the rich potential that Deleuzian cartography holds for revolutionizing curriculum practice and teacher education. The data serve as a foil for the power of the concepts, the wall which theory must meet.

Notes

1. In *Difference and Repetition*, Deleuze explains that difference is "tamed" by subjecting it to the "four iron collars of representation: identity in the concept, opposition in the predicate, analogy in judgement and resemblance in perception" (262). In other words, in Platonic or representational thinking, difference is allowed to be thought of only as conceptual difference and so on, but not as difference in itself. Two identical objects share the same concept and yet are different.

2. In one sense, singularities are poised states of systems that are the result of the architecture of forces being set up in a certain way, which makes for the arising of certain nodal points and not others. That is to say, certain point intensities arise or are synthesized due to a particular distribution of forces in the social field. To give a concrete

example, many commentators hold that the systematic undermining of the treaty of Versailles that led to the armistice in the Second World War created the atmosphere for the rise of Nazism in postwar Germany. Singularities are also multiplicities since they can change into alternative states by being pushed over a certain threshold by surrounding forces.

3. Fractals are in-between, non-whole dimensions that emerge out of endlessly proliferating subdivisions of a system such as a coastline. Technically, they demonstrate the profound fact that the measures of things depend on the scale used for measurement. A coastline from A to B appears as limited, definite, and bounded when seen from a large-scale perspective. On a smaller scale, the irregularities multiply in a countless manner.

4. To return to our earlier example about religion, student and teacher arrive at a much better position to deal with the signifying systems of religion as well as liberal secularism. In fact, such investigation leads to a more profound inquiry when it is seen that the foundational figures of religions often belonged to no religion, each having walked away from the earlier faith or the respective "molar" categories to become truly nomadic, but who were, nevertheless, profoundly religious. So the order-word religion cannot capture the excess that is religiosity. Similarly, it can be shown that the slogan of "secularism" is connected to a network of presuppositions. This way we extract the molecular singularities of religiosity and secularism from their bounded categories.

5. For instance, by pronouncing a substance as illegal it becomes immediately proscribed, but this is only possible with the excess or surplus value that the legal system generates, and not by the nature of the substance itself. Or, by pronouncing two people as man and wife, a whole set of social obligations and codes are suddenly placed around the couple.

6. The *planomenon* is a term used by Deleuze and Guattari to indicate a mode of composition that holds together disparate and divergent elements through states of intensity rather than any intrinsic similarity. They sometimes refer to it also as the *plane of consistency*.

7. Molecularization is a return to premolar formations, that is, to the singular or the plane of intensities that cannot be divided into individualities. The singular is not a bounded unity but a multiplicity, a condition, a state of things, an hour of the day, a pitch of tension.

8. The plane of continual variation is another way of talking about the plane of consistency described in Note 6 above. It is a plane of intensities rather than individualizations.

Chapter 2

An Outline of the Case Study

It is through loss, rather than acquisition, that one progresses and picks up speed.   —Deleuze and Guattari, *A Thousand Plateaus*

Here I will make a transition to the case study, to an introduction that cannot be deferred any longer. The link, if the reader cares to hold on to it, is the map. The previous sections attempted to construct a cartography of the Deleuzian ontology and pragmatics that remapped the differentials subsumed by thought onto an alternative set of empiricist coordinates. The Deleuzian map is at once politics, art, philosophy, and social theory, and helps us move between the "rigid formations of the state, the unconscious, [and] language" (Kaufman, 1998, 5) and the tumult of experience, making it invaluable for navigating the structure of an institution like school, which lies at the intersection of these formations.

And besides, the map is not merely navigational, but is also productive. When several maps are projected onto one another, we have what Deleuze calls a diagram. This diagram is in a continuous process of becoming:

A diagram is a map, or rather several superimposed maps. And from one diagram to the next, new maps are drawn. Thus there is no diagram that does not also include, besides the points which it connects up, certain relatively free or unbound points, points of creativity, change and resistance. (44)

By several superimposed maps—living configurations of forces—I will try to create a picture of the flows and blockages of the terrain under investigation. And the very act of superposition will allow us to construct new layers of connection to Deleuzian concepts.

Let us begin with an excerpt from the Case Journal:

> Arnie emerges out of an obscure door along North Street's scruffy, brick-lined buildings, and ambles down the cold, windy street to the bus stop. A few dry leaves, remnants from the fall, swirl around him. He huddles in one corner of the shelter and fumbles in his pocket for the city bus pass. Arnie has just left his *placement* for the day, and is heading back to The City School for his afternoon "in-house" science class. He has spent most of the morning at a Women, Infants, and Children (WIC) distribution center weighing and checking out the case histories of infants, and distributing vouchers that mothers can exchange for infant food. This is a part of his school internship called placement.
>
> Arnie does not get paid for the work at the WIC but gets school credit toward his graduation, an event which seemed a very remote possibility six months ago. Near the end of his junior year, Arnie had been expelled from one of the city's high schools. According to Arnie, his expulsion was the result of a series of difficulties, constant fights, ethnic tension, and gang activity that he got into during that year. Thinking over it all during the summer, Arnie realized that he simply had to get back to school, but he found that given his situation, alternative schools were his only option. But he wanted no part of alternative schools. It was his father who first told him about The City School, and together they paid a visit to the school's lead teacher, M.S., to make enquiries. M.S. was skeptical about Arnie's ability to work in the community without supervision, but Arnie's persuasiveness won the day and he got his second chance. Talking about his experience, Arnie says, "I learned more in the first nine weeks here than I did in all of high school." (Journal Entry No.11)

The City School is in no small measure a remarkable place, an evaluation that someone like Arnie would agree with wholeheartedly. The group of teachers who founded the school did not form a charter, but applied to start a school within the district public school system, under a scheme called the Innovative Schools Program, floated in order to invite new ideas for catering to difference, that is, for responding to different needs of urban adolescents.

At the time I began visiting the school, it was entering its eighth year of existence. District reports on The City School showed high level of attendance (93 percent) and graduation (90 percent) rates in a district with a truancy rate of 40 percent and an equally high dropout rate. A Regional Educational Laboratory report (NCREL, 1998) also stated that the innovative schools "outperformed their district peers on the whole," achieving "Board Standards on seven indicators, while the district as a whole achieved standards on two" (3). While the statistics were impressive, it was the sense of a somewhat altered space that made me want to get involved in what the school was doing for young people, find out how it was doing what it was doing, the kind of people that took on this challenge, and the demand the school placed on its teachers.

Preliminary visits showed that the school had, since its inception, distinguished itself in many ways. Its raison d'etre was to establish a different space. A group of teachers had decided to provide a very different atmosphere than the "faceless and hostile buildings [mainstream urban schools] where thousands are held" and where "students have to switch off certain parts of their humanity in order to survive." They wanted to create a place where "you did not need to look over your shoulder in order to feel safe." (Field Notes 02/05/02, and excerpts from interviews with teachers)

Also, the founding teachers did not want hierarchy. They rejected the usual separation between teaching and administration, and felt that the two realms were really inseparable, especially in the kind of school they wanted. One of the older teachers explained that by creating a division between teaching and administering "the work of the educator is fragmented…[the school] becomes like a factory." (Field Notes 02/11/02) Another problem some felt was that this caused zones to appear where neither was responsible, for instance, neither was responsible for the *whole* child. Therefore, The City School, although a public school, and not a charter, decided to become a teacher-run school.

This has a large impact on the nature of the terrain in which school relations articulate themselves. Looking through a Deleuzian lens, I saw it demonstrating some inchoate elements of what Deleuze and

Guattari call "smooth space" (Deleuze and Guattari, 1987, 474–75). As a quick contrast, smooth space is to "striated space" as fabric is to felt. Fabric is closely governed, has verticals and horizontals, and is closed by the warp of the loom. It serves as a good example of regulated or administered spaces that are vertically ordered, that is, have a top and a bottom. Felt, on the other hand, is nomadic or smooth; it is produced by the entanglement of millions of microfibers oriented in every direction—it is an accumulation of proximities all at the same level, making it nonhierarchical.

At least in its setup, The City School was nonhierarchical; it was not embedded in a higher or supplemental dimension; that is to say, the pedagogic plane was not nested within a separately administered space, but was its own space, which is characteristic of smooth spaces in that it saturates the plane. The cartography of Deleuze and Guattari activates "a method that dehierarchizes the building blocks...and reassembles them in a different and more elemental state" (Kaufman, 1998, 7). The refusal of a supplemental or superior dimension helps to open up the potentialities that would otherwise remain locked up in boundary constructs, and a certain careful and intensive articulation of the refusal can reorient experience toward new pedagogic openings. In other words, it is a first step toward a pedagogy of immanence.

Not only did the teachers at this school want to build a different atmosphere, but the objective was also to offer a curriculum that was much more suited to the needs of urban youth whose lives were rather complex, many of whom had to support themselves and their families from an early age, had no regular homes, lived in unsafe neighborhoods, and among whom teenage pregnancy, drug problems and dropout rates were high. One teacher recounts making a home visit to meet the parents of a particularly obstinate youth: "I was getting ready to knock on the door, when I found that there was no door, only an opening where a door should have been." (Conversations, Field Notes, 03/19/02) Suppressing a desire to escape, he went in to find that there were no adults living under that roof. The fifteen-year-old was the sole occupant along with a sister who was also a minor, in a house that had no door. The question had to be asked: How must curriculum respond to these rather unusual conditions? And the fact is that such questions do get asked at the school, which keeps open its innovative character.

The building in which The City School is housed is not very different from Arnie's placement that was described earlier. It is at one end of downtown where the banks and prosperous businesses taper off, and empty parking lots and closed storefronts take their place. At the street level there are shops and eateries, and the elevator takes you up to the fifth floor where you step out directly into the lobby of the school. The ceiling is low and the walls are white and clean, with large sections covered by notices and display boards. The long corridor makes sharply angled turns and opens into a series of classrooms on either side. Most of the classrooms are generous in size and have large windows. Because there is a great shortage of space, there is no library in the school, and the students use the public library, which is only a couple of blocks away, as their library resource. There are no science labs or other auxiliary facilities in the place either.

The City School's curriculum was organized by fusing two broad curricular strategies. One was the "city-as-school" model that originated in the New School for Social Sciences; it involved bringing in the issues of urban life into the school as much as possible, and taking the school beyond the physical walls back into the city. The idea was that the students must not be trapped within walls of the classroom for too long and pursue their learning into the life around them that included educational field visits.

The second model brought into the picture was the idea of service learning, that is, learning through experience, whose roots can be traced all the way back to Dewey. Service Learning is structured around placements that put students in the community in a work-learning situation. Placements are located in enterprises ranging from law offices to elementary schools to community health centers. The teacher (also called the resource coordinator here) supervising the student in the placement must write a curriculum for each placement that reflects the type of work in which the student is engaged. So the teacher is also a curriculum developer, which is important to note. This individualized, placement-specific curriculum is called a Learning Experience Activity Packet (LEAP), and is supplied to the student by the teacher/resource coordinator. The packet consists of a series of assignments or projects related to the placement. LEAPs are due at the end of every nine-week cycle.

Besides being supervised by the resource coordinator, students are also mentored by personnel at the cooperating placements. These individuals help plan learning goals and activities, and see that the agreement to provide the student with a meaningful learning experience is fulfilled. Occasionally, a placement turns out to be vacuous in terms of meaningful learning, in which case it is dropped after a periodic review. The cooperating resource records the student's attendance and assesses students' growth and learning as part of an evaluation report. The students do not receive payment for this work but are granted one-fourth credit toward their graduation for every thirty-six hours worked at a placement.

The students indicate that the placements are a big reason that the school has worked for them. "Our placements depend a lot on us, expect a lot from us...and we have placements where we can usually learn new things," one student observed. Another said, "They know that I can do the job." The sense of reliance and responsibility seems to play a big part in the relationship between placements and the students. Supporting this view, the school program coordinator says, "Having them [students] out in the community does a lot for their self-images a lot of the time. Also, it's good for the community to know that these kids are okay." (Field Notes 04/05/02 and Interview excerpt)

While placements are a key feature of The City School curriculum, the students also enroll in other core classes at the school, which meets the state and district competency and proficiency standards. The options are not too many but the science, math, and language courses are all there. As for the "Advanced Placement" courses, the students take them online with support from the staff. Students also enroll in university courses to get college credit. Recently, the students voted to learn Latin when a slot opened up for including an additional course.

Innovative schools typically tend to be small. This one is a high school with around a hundred and fifty students, of whom nearly 70 percent are African Americans, 7 percent Hispanics, 15 percent Whites, and the rest Asians and Native Americans. A majority of these students are described as being "at-risk." Many of them had dropped out of school at one time or another and had found their way to this place. The school has ten staff members in all, roughly balanced in race and gender composition.

A four-tier structure exists for governing The City School. The School Advisory Board represents broad and diverse community interests. It meets quarterly and oversees the link between the community and the program. Board input guides and informs the overarching goals of the school and brings in issues of change in the urban community. Next, the Board of Directors, composed of school faculty, parents, and resource site representatives, oversees operations of the school. The group meets monthly and through its site-based management orientation monitors the school's activities and provides support where necessary. Third, day-to-day decision-making occurs at weekly staff meetings. Decision-making takes place through consensus. Finally, a Student Council composed of student volunteers sees to the more student-centered, day-to-day interests of the school, such as planning field trips and other activities.

The Problematic
The history of innovations shows that such innovations as I am talking about often tend to have a limited life; after an initial period during which there is a burst of enthusiasm, there is a tendency to get reabsorbed into the mainstream due to internal differences, funding difficulties, problems with facilities, and so on. This tends to happen frequently when the founders retire or the original group fragments and new group members join; the power of the original vision begins to dilute and fade and the school falls back into the general mass from which it had distinguished itself.

The City School is precisely at this critical juncture now. My concern is that in the process of falling back into the sea like a spent rocket, the considerable positive gains made, and insights achieved, are lost to the educational community. It is important that the appetite for change and reform actively take into account the significant work that happens in such places without attempting to use it as a cookie-cutter model, nor pushing it aside as a one-of-a-kind experiment. Instead, it would profit the educational community to develop an active relationship with such innovative moves as can be positively identified. The City School is struggling to find out how to resist the gravitational pull of the middle: "The vultures are always circling overhead, waiting to rub us out....Every year it is a battle, the big schools say, 'We could do with those funds, what on earth are they doing.' Internal resistance, that's key to our survival," M.S., a lead teacher observed (Interview with M.S. No.1). Internal resistance involves realization of the power of difference and innovation at all levels within the school, and an important part of this is the perception of new teachers.

For one of the major sources from which such a centripetal tendency toward the "Same" and the elimination of difference comes is from the direction of fresh induction of teachers. M.S. tells me,

> Soon there will be only myself and two others left of the original group. Unless the incoming teachers learn how to run this place, do the placements and things the school will slide...maybe close down. All the innovative places I know are having trouble with their new hires. Most of them simply don't understand how these places work. (Interview with M.S. No.1)

There are powerful reasons for this. First, as we have discussed in the previous chapter, teachers bring with them their conventional expectations or boundary constructs of what a teacher's job entails. Second, teacher education programs rarely take into account innovative programs and their very different needs. Also, new faculty often do not have much of an appreciation of the original imperatives and the struggles the school has gone through, nor do they fully comprehend the vision of the founders. *Innovativeness can survive only on further innovation*, at every turn, thereby avoiding stagnation and assimilation. A disciplined and operational grasp of this generative principle requires the release of certain resources, as well as ways of thinking and being, that are not often the focus of teacher preparation. Specifically, at The City School, the problem was to draw out the novice teachers' energies without subordinating them to a fixed vision, as well as to maintain a critical line of flight without compromising the very purpose of the innovation.

As the reader will observe, I have narrowed down the problem to that of teacher induction without falling into representational structures—a question of bringing the two, novice teacher and existing innovative program, together without disabling either. One way this seems possible is through operationalizing the Deleuzian concept of becoming. In brief, the pragmatics of becoming, of which I speak at length later in the book, is the continual reconstellation of sense data, in conjunction with other bodies, to yield new formations that do not fit any representational schema. I argue that the core of innovativeness lies in becoming, and the praxis that I suggest in the rest of the book involves such a becoming on the part of the teachers.

The radical implications of this go far beyond the current context, for although the problem relates to a specific case, Wolcott (1994) observes that "complex specificness," while heightening circumstantiality, may reveal implications and relevance to a broader context (98). There is nothing particularly new in the statement that schools are not static, but dynamic or evolving entities. But what I want to suggest here is something different: It is that schools, especially those like The City School, must operate as *becoming* structures. The difference being that becoming does not involve going from point A to point B, as the term *evolving* might imply. Instead, becoming generates new and irregular spaces of proliferating connections that have important consequences for the harnessing of new forces. But it also means preparing teachers to enter those spaces in productive ways.

Talking to Teachers
While my conversations with teachers continue through the rest of the chapters, I am going to introduce some of the data here as a prelude that will give us a preliminary sense of the situation. Along with the data, I will simultaneously start the work of unfolding the conceptual series in a preliminary sort of way, allowing many of these issues to crop up again later in the book. It is important to keep in mind that the data are exemplary in the main, and rather than driving the work, are used mostly to explicate the Deleuzian approach.

In my conversations, I frequently find concern on the part of the older faculty regarding the issue of induction of new staff. Interestingly, in the early meetings I attended, the talk was about how the new teachers will "fit in" with the existing setup. In subsequent references to this issue, the question became "How do we integrate new staff?" More recently, the question has further evolved into "How can we work together?" This last has also come about with the realization on the part of the school staff as a group that they will have to be responsible for their own staff development in ways that they had previously not considered. As I have mentioned before, this is due to the fact that mainstream teacher preparation does little for innovative or small-school situations, and it is a folly to think that these are reduced-scale versions of mainstream schools. Here we need teachers who are educated and willing to innovate.

Discussing novice teachers, M.S., who is a social studies teacher in his early fifties, and now a lead teacher, comments:

> They usually tend to be managerial. In one of the other schools they are having trouble with one of their new hires. He believes in confrontation, suspending kids…you know…We are beginning to get some of that too, but that is not what we are all about. It changes the codes of the place.

In the language of our analysis, order-words like suspension or discipline are connected to a whole hierarchy of presuppositions that remain silent. Instead, molar categories attempt to establish control through layers of fictive alliances that work to exclude the "stutterings" and "murmurs" within a situation. To my question as to why he thought they tend to be managerial, M.S. responds,

> Places like this are hard. The kids range from overeffusiveness [laughs] to total indifference. Their backgrounds are very complicated and our educational assumptions and ideas of what they need are simplistic…To come to terms with all that is a first step. But the first impulse is to control and the kids react to that. (Interview with M.S. No.1)

Not listening to the "murmurs" makes our approach to curriculum "simplistic," as we operate within the redundancies of established strata. The murmurs contain rich and dense curricular material studiously ignored by the official curriculum. I ask M.S. whether he thinks teacher education programs can help new teachers orient themselves differently, and confront these tendencies in any systematic manner. M.S. seems doubtful: "It's a very different tack we are talking about…what could be done other than somehow find the right people?" he muses. (Interview with M.S. No.1)

Next I speak to L.S., one of the novice teachers who mentions some of her difficulties at The City School:

> K.R.: Tell me about your sense of this place and how you have meshed with it.

L.S.: I have never done scheduling for students or the writing of curriculum. In the schools I have worked in, the students get their schedules from wherever…Here I am having to learn very different things.

K.R.: Do you see these aspects as outside the scope of teaching?

L.S.: Well, mostly they take up a lot of time. I feel I have less time for teaching. Although students can actually choose and write up their schedules but I had to learn how to keep track of them all.

K.R.: What has been the most troublesome aspect?

L.S.: I have never seen a placement before or worked at going out and creating a new placement or internship. That is a whole new skill one has to learn. It means going out into the community and convincing people. And each student's learning program has to be written up around the Placement. I feel a little overwhelmed at this point, but I'm sure I will get used to it, it is still all very new. (Interview with L.S. No.1)

Seen from a conventional perspective, there is nothing startling in L.S.'s comments—a novice teacher gradually adjusting to her new situation. But here is an important issue: Innovation is not an old structure adapting to a new one, nor even a new one repeating itself. L.S. is proceeding in a category-bound manner, seeing herself and the apparently linear tasks before her as two irreducible formations that confront each other. But in Deleuzian terms, what we really have is an interface as a result of a set of intensities that bear down on another set, or rather, on each other, defining a field of relations that is anything but linear. Setting up the analysis in these terms helps to get at the emerging singularities of each moment rather than seeing the situation as a unified problem.

Another teacher, A.D., from West Africa, and with a background of having taught advanced programs in science in one of the city's well-known schools, came to The City School because he was looking for something new.

A.D.: I wanted a change and I knew some teachers here, and they said, come on over and try this place if you want a change, you are sure going to get it. And they were right.

K.R.: Is this the change you had hoped for?

A.D.: Well, this *is* different. The student is allowed to take charge of how much they want to learn. But for new teachers like me, it is a *big* change.

K.R.: Will you please explain that?

A.D.: There are aspects about which I am not always sure. How does the Learning Experience Activity actually work? Does it work? How can we maintain attendance in this place? How to develop resources? There are many new adjustments to be made. Student class size is another issue—these are small classes—how to teach multilevel students? (Interview with A.D. Nos.1 and 2)

From my conversations with A.D., it is apparent that he seeks some kind of pedagogical meaning in the place that will give it a certain coherence, a stable system that he was used to; that, in other words, will nail it for him. But meaning, according to Deleuze, does not lie in the particularity or genesis of a thing or place. Instead, it is a passage or an interface between two force fields. The content, or force field called curriculum, never really meets the expression, or function field called teacher/student; their relation is asymptotic. To put it differently, contrary to the commonplace belief that there is a meeting between student and the curriculum, in this mode of analysis we find that these two series, or regimes of organization, are so unlike each other that it is impossible to localize the point of such correspondence; and it is reasonable therefore, although startling, to come to the conclusion that there never is any meeting ground or correspondence between them.

What occurs, instead, is that each cause breaks up into multiple causes, and there is a continual fracturing as every point turns fractal, the teacher's translations, the past-future of the present moment, the hour of the day, last night's lack of sleep, the particular organization of knowledge in the text, testing, and a myriad of micro-events that interpose themselves between the two series. How are these two series, say, the child and the curriculum, then to correspond with each other? It happens not through correspondence but through what Deleuze calls an "abstract machine," a statistical selection from an infinitude of forces and unformed matter that move back and forth creating what we normally call meaning (Deleuze and Guattari, 1987, 511). This back-and-forth movement cannot be fully captured by any representational system. Thus, Massumi (1992) observes:

> If meaning is a process of translation from one substance to another of a different order and back again, what it moves across is an unbridgeable abyss of fracturing. If meaning is the in-between of content and expression, it is nothing more (nor less) than their "nonrelation." (16)

In other words, the "meaning" of the educational encounter lies not in the capacity to produce a unified sensibility, but in its paradoxical capacity to *deal with nonrelation*, or in placing itself in the "in-between" of content and expression. This in-betweenness or the gap or nonrelation is neither vague nor confusing, but is an access to the myriad forces and intensities that constantly cross our path but that are ignored as we adhere to narrow ideas about curriculum.

I treat the school's attempts to innovate very seriously here as an index of the promised accommodation of difference. Consequently, I try to find ways that innovation can find new lines of flight here. To reiterate, innovation is not a structure that is repeated, but a progressive differentiation that alone can enter, through slippage, the in-between spaces. Innovation is the lateral insertion of a space of becoming that is not metric in the sense of measurable, and yet rigorous in terms of effects. It must take place within the confines of the district rules and guidelines, and yet produce novel effects in thought and curriculum. It is important to note that both LS and AD start out by perceiving difference not as an opening to innovate, that is, not as a positivity, but as a lack, as something they have never countenanced before, and hence threatening. This notion of a lack or deficiency, as Deleuze and Guattari repeatedly observe in their works, is one of the most deeply ingrained formations in thought.

Also, G.M., an older teacher, thinks that novice teachers sometimes place too much emphasis on the distinctness of the tasks:

> The problem is that these are not separate skills that some of us possess. They are part of a certain approach to students…it comes out of that.

What kind of approach? I press him.

> Well, some of us would fight for them to get educated…and they know that. We try to do what is necessary. All this is taxing, I

admit, but the school remains open to these kids only so long as each one of us is prepared to do the necessary. (Interview with G.M. No.2)

G.M. seems to imply that what it takes to educate these kids is not so much a list of skills as a certain mode of perception—a *gestalt*. A second point is that innovation or creating novelty in approaches, methods, relations, and content must occur at all points for the school to remain innovative. And yet, G.M. does not go far enough from the perspective of a Deleuzian schema. For if it is true that innovation is not mere progression, but a more radical movement, then desire cannot remain confined to educating "those kids." For then we are leaving the teacher as an unquestioned molar category. While it is certainly necessary to educate the kids, G.M. needs to be pushed to consider going beyond the "Other," in the direction of a more nomadic topos for true innovation. And in order to release the full power of a Deleuzian cartography, we have to go after the singularities, instead of the molar categories, that hold back too much in the way of binding energy in the boundary constructs.

In operational terms, this means that one must loosen the molar division between the teacher and the taught, and learn to look at the field as emerging points of intensity. It does not mean that teachers abandon their adult roles and responsibilities; it simply means they invoke their molecular multiplicities within the unifying category, and enter the curriculum as a becoming to combine with singularities or traits that make up the molar category called student. Every point-intensity or singularity in that field must proliferate in connections, and not merely aim to affect the category called student. It is not so much about educating those kids, as much as educating the *field of relations* that includes the kids, teacher, and the environment. To put it differently, the students' learning can better emerge *in relation with* the teacher's struggle against the tendency toward molarization. This is not a holistic perspective, but a proliferation of multiplicities, or entry into fractal dimensions.

I ask K.C., another teacher new to The City School, who has "substituted" in several schools in the district, what distinguished this place as compared with the other places where she had worked:

K.C.: This place is small and you work much closer with the kids.

And things like mentoring, for example, which is important here.
K.R.: What kind of different effort does it involve to do that?
K.C.: I don't know that it is some additional thing, but there's lots
of things taken for granted which you find out gradually.
K.R.: Can you give me an example?
K.C.: Well, teachers are expected to keep track of individual
students. Many students have had problems in the past. Close
mentoring rarely happens in large places. Also there are
consequences. If the kids goof off in the placements, they close
the door on us. The community comes to know…there is always
this pressure of things outside your control. (Interview with K.C.
No. 1)

The notion of control, and the uneasiness over uncertainty, underlies
some of the key constructs of mainstream pedagogical practices (see
Doll, 2002). Therefore, it is not surprising to hear K.C. express concern
that things at the school seem somewhat out of control because of the
outside coming in constantly as students come in from the field. In
Deleuzian terms, the minimizing of uncertainty is the work of the
State machinery, whose main goal in education is the manufacturing
of docile bodies that are predictable.

In Deleuze there is always an aleatory "Outside" from where forces
suddenly appear—forces of deterritorialization that destabilize and
cannot be fully controlled. These are not to be shunned; they produce
new lines of thought. In a school that embraces a city-as-school
curricular model, we are likely to see more of these forces from the
outside. Rather than resisting these, we have to establish in teachers a
mode of being and thinking that sees the pedagogical potential of
these lines of force. The connectivities thus produced expand and
construct piecemeal a Deleuzian patchwork curriculum, extending in
all directions in the manner of a quilt.

To verify my observations, I ask an experienced teacher, N.C., what
special nature of adaptive moves novice teachers could make in terms
of becoming more attuned to the place:

N.C.: Politically, this place works a little differently. Also, you
know, older staff have a shared vision that is hard sometimes to
communicate. Our ways often come out of that vision. This is not
necessarily a difficult place to work in, but you have to get close

to the kids, and there is an enormous burden...too many things going on in their lives. There is a frustration sometimes in not doing enough. Also there is a lot of uncertainty here. You never know what the district is going to do.

K.R.: How do new teachers cope with this?

N.C.: For those who stay on things begin to change after a while. But you can also protect yourself by not getting involved, and some choose that route. But there is a price to be paid for that too. (Interview with N.C. No.2)

The task of the teacher here is multiplicitous; not in the sense of the conventional duality of many versus one, but each one an irreducible multiplicity. As Bains (2002) has pointed out, Deleuze's multiplicity is not a numeric multiplicity; instead, it is a "qualitative multiplicity involving duration as one of its conditions. A qualitative multiplicity is not an aggregate of parts constituted by the relation of separate physical existents but an event, an actual occasion of experience. A processual pathic intensity" (104). A qualitative multiplicity is like density or temperature—it is an intensity or intensive property that cannot be divided up like space or volume. It is an event, and is not an aggregate, just as the learning encounter, in which the various elements—student and teacher—exist only in reciprocal presupposition and cannot be separated. The event is not happening to each of them, but *they are the event*.

Not to start from identity but from qualitative multiplicity is a very different way of relating to the world. To recall one of Deleuze and Guattari's fundamental theses, entities are generated from a pre-individual autopoietic or self-referential node of events and intensive singularities that are themselves multiplicities brought about through tendencies generated in the microphysics of contractions and contemplations. Such a view alters the nature of space from an optic visionality that sees things as points and numerical multiplicities to what Deleuze and Guattari have called a tactile space, that is, a space in which orientation is by means of intensive or indivisible properties of continuous variation (Deleuze and Guattari, 1987, 492). In such a space, one does not remain outside the event, but becomes implicated in the plane of the event, emerging as part of a constellation of forces. Pedagogy on this plane has a very different implication; it means moving from a *theorematic* stance with appeals to universals, to a more *problematic* one that considers the specificity of each encounter as a new becoming. Admittedly, peeling off layers of strata, dispositions, or habits of thought is not a simple matter; it needs a concerted effort at the combined level of affect, concept, and percept.

Thus, the significant strand in what I was observing and what I wish to comment on here is the ways in which new teachers, whether new to the profession or to the innovative environment, came together with the school that seemed to throw up some unique problems of practice for the entrants. The difficulties faced by these teachers, as observed by me, are grouped below under certain categories in order to facilitate the work of analysis.

Analytical Categories

From a certain meditation on the interview data as well as observations, some patterns emerged of the difficulties novice teachers faced in encountering the more open environment. I have cast these problems as effects of the confrontation with the incipient nomadic situation at the school with its fissures and "irregularities." These latencies, together with the semiotics and the necessary lines of praxis, are more thoroughly discussed in the chapters that follow. Here, an opening move is made in the direction of analysis; I revisit these in depth subsequently.

Using Deleuzian cartography, I have grouped the latencies I noticed in terms of five overlapping categories of spatial characteristics as follows: 1. Smoothness; 2. Multiplicity; 3. Rhizoidness; 4. In-Betweenness; and 5. Becoming. Taken together, these traits open up lines of continuous variation of nomadic space that deterritorializes the categories and boundaries within which conventional approaches to curriculum operate. My observation is that The City School exhibited certain nomadic fissures and openings, but the novice teachers I observed, being prepared within mainstream conventions, were not helped to recognize these as generative traits that could overcome some of the difficulties they faced in educating urban youth. The categories discussed below are not just the problems, but also probings about theorizing these spaces, that is, recuperating the existing positive latencies in a theoretical mold in order to strengthen them operationally. In other words, we want to influence them in ways that the useful tendencies become actualized in stronger ways. An autopoiesis or self-generation can be the outcome.

1. Smoothness. Smooth space is open-ended; it allows one to move from any point to any other point with the least amount of resistance. It is also a space of intensities constructed through a proliferation of connections. As I have remarked earlier, the organization of The City School appeared to have elements of smooth space, owing to a reduction of hierarchy, that is, strata, and the possibility of constantly creating new curricular material through the LEAPs, that is, the possibilities of making new connections. As a teacher run school, it has no separate administration, and on account of the absence of a supplementary or "higher" dimension within the operations of the school, most problems cannot transcend, but must be flattened out and dealt with on the pedagogical plane. While one of the senior teachers carries out the administrative role as a lead teacher, the role circulates, and decisions are made jointly.

Teachers coming from a mainstream perspective, who are used to the clear separation of teaching from administration, tend to find a) the lack of central authority, or the absence of an Oedipal figure, generally unnerving; b) more specifically, that the absence of such a figure of interdiction, to whom one can send a difficult student, or whose proxy one can use as a deterrent, made functioning more difficult; and c) that they were wanting in the skills of dialogue that are necessary for the joint decision-making process that must replace administrative authority.

In terms of flattening out the disciplinary dimension onto the pedagogical plane, my data suggest that beginning teachers often come in with certain persistent technocratic metaphors that drive teacher behavior, one of which is "classroom management." Now, to think in terms of management, in the context of learning, is to think of apparatuses of control and stratification that seek to eliminate disorder by taking refuge in sameness and identity. But innovative schools such as The City School work to operate along different lines with regard to such issues. Instead of the compliance, control, and confrontation paradigm, which springs from the traditional vision of adults as legislators and students as subjects, small schools such as this one attempt to create an atmosphere of close interpersonal relationships that tend to obviate the need for harsh disciplinary measures by opening up lines of communication. Occasional wayward behavior tends to be seen as a signal for help rather than an isolated problem. For new teachers, the move to get away from the "classroom management and discipline" mind-set takes considerable work and revisioning of what it means to work with adolescents. It partly means discovering the pedagogical possibilities of irregular spaces and the positivity of difference, as well as perceiving the need for breaking down categories. This part of the analysis is taken up in detail along with field data in the following chapter.

2. Multiplicity. Teachers play not a multiple but a multiplicity of roles at The City School. The teacher is not just an instructor but also a curriculum developer, a placement guide, and a mentor. But each of these are also composed of the others, and cannot be fully separated. The fact that the students are out in the community part of the time changes the dynamics of the school, requiring teachers to be more inventive about their roles as well as make connections between field experience and school. This is not only with respect to the formal aspects of the field experience, but also with respect to students bringing with them attitudes and experiences that arise from being out there that result in a certain divergence and proliferation of differences. Connections have therefore to be made between the different sites. There is thus a continual three-way interplay between school, community, and curriculum that emerge out of this process.

But it is precisely this switching of roles that is often the most difficult act for novice teachers, especially when they come with fixed conceptions about teacher roles. One of the most difficult parts some felt was the role of placement guide. This involves overseeing student's actions in the community. Conventional categories, and boundaries around the teacher's role, thus tend to loosen up somewhat at The City School, and the demand is for a level of flexibility and ability to deal with contingency for which newcomers are often unprepared.

I hope to show in subsequent discussions that a Deleuzian reconceptualization of the pedagogical encounter in terms of events and multiplicities is very helpful, as it tends to dislodge us from fixed ways of thinking, and helps us to see the emergent properties and variations that produce multiplicities. It is not that by emphasizing multiplicity teachers are being asked to give up their identities in some mindless form of collectivity. On the contrary, we are enabled, by means of this radical eco-ontology, to straddle the plane of molar identity as well as the plane of microidentity or molecularity. This tension between the two series produces resonance of productive ambiguity that can generate a new thought. Instead of a pre-formatted coherence in curriculum, the emphasis then shifts to producing connections between different nodes in a contingent fashion. The view of identity as multiplicity allows us to enter a different relationship with the plane of composition out of which curriculum emerges like an event, and breaks down traditional roles. In an environment that shows a latent multiplicity, theorizing in this manner increases the chances of strengthening the autopoietic or self-generational possibilities of concepts.

3. Rhizoidness. The "rhizome" is a lateral proliferation of connections, like the spread of moss, the sudden branching off or joining up of different intensities, flows, and densities to form new assemblies that have no fixed form or outline. A contingent mass, the rhizome can be cut up in any way and still retains operational wholeness; therefore it is highly tenacious. The rhizome is also a tuber, and unlike ordinary roots, can sprout in any direction.

The success of a place like The City School depends to a large extent on the ways each player finds or invents channels and bands of communication both within and without the school, that is, between student and teacher, teachers and parents, the school and the district, or among teachers themselves. Apart from the fact that in a school that is jointly run by teachers, much hinges on the ways in which the players construct "rhizoid" lines among one another that increases the proliferation of intricate connectivity, increasing thereby the chances of survival. Further, the fact of being different from mainstream schools, and the effort to protect this difference itself, calls for the creation of various continuums of intensities and variations.

Besides normal instruction, teachers also have to monitor the students at their work places, finding ways of individually assessing the work each student does at the placement through the LEAPs. Difficulties often crop up at the placements which have to be smoothed out. Liaising between multiple sites, the successful placement coordinator has to project continuously a forward-looking agenda that keeps all parties positively engaged. Each of these requires a degree of sophistication in communicative abilities that is atypical of average teaching situations. Conceived in rhizospheric terms, such activity, instead of being seen as fragmented bits in isolated spaces, can be reconceptualized as connecting up points of intensities that together form different plateaus. A redescription of this nature strengthens the operational and conceptual strength of the space, as well as increases the range of the pragmatics of action by proliferating the combinations of these point intensities. It is the principle of pulling up by the bootstraps, or self-generation; it takes what is present, and feeding it into the theoretical framework, lets a new level of intensity emerge.

Even instruction tends to have a somewhat different emphasis. My data show that the teachers who are successful with students at The City School, that is, who are considered to have made a difference in some of their lives, invariably are those who have taken a step beyond their more circumscribed teacherly roles and taken a special interest in students' lives. It would be easy to jump to the explanatory device of pastoral care and its positive effects, but discussions with teachers give glimpses of another movement, a becoming in teachers' lives not usually accounted for. Here, Deleuzian theory can play a powerful role by making a distinction between standard explanations such as pastoral care and a rhizomatic mode where it is not a question of hierarchical giving, nor even of growth, but the becoming of a multiplicity.

4. In-betweenness. The sense one has at the school is that of being in between things. Students are often in between the field and the classroom, the teachers are in between observing the placements and teaching in-house classes. In-betweenness here is everywhere. It is also a state of emergent things; it can be viewed as a relationality that is always beyond determinate boundaries. This latency not only remains undertheorized at the school, which, while it displays some of these qualities has yet to draw rigorous pedagogical praxis from it, but novice teachers also find the qualities of in-betweenness discomforting.

To take in-betweenness not as a passage to something more definite but to treat it seriously, as an open space within every process, we have to understand how the teacher can act from the middle, from the in-between spaces, neither unifying instruction nor offering discrete packets aimed at different "individuals." Instead, the task is to construct a plane—Deleuze would call it a plane of consistency—which draws out all the unformed elements, and show the fields of indefinitude or flux in which they are embedded. To take an example, in the teaching of history, in-betweenness destroys the linearity and opens it up as a space of nonlinear becoming. No level is closed, and all the unformed elements at each level only excite, attract, and free up elements at other levels, making aggregates that are fuzzy and yet rigorous. At any point in time, the class is thus a rhizome, stretching and contracting between different point intensities, never unifying, nor becoming disparate. And the teacher's position is always in-between, dancing between the lines. Under such circumstances the emphasis moves from the unifying of curricular levels, topics, and ideas to seeing/constructing/inventing new connections between them, and thereby also multiplying the pedagogical directions from which to tackle an issue.

There is also another angle to this from the perspective of the whole school. The bottom line for innovative schools is an ever-present need for a degree of creative enterprise. Because it is small, unusual, and surviving against enormous odds, The City School staff must continually improvise. They must make decisions that no one else can make for them. They are a square peg in a round hole; the district rules regarding attendance, assessment, or school hours do not fit them, making it necessary to remain on the witness stand. Therefore, at every turn there is the in-betweenness of being an innovative place. But these can also become part of the pedagogy, and need not remain isolated from it. The school has yet to utilize these instabilities and indeterminacies as pedagogic openings, although the possibilities are there. Beginning teachers can enter the plane of composition, keeping their eye on this line of tension between the school and its immediate context.

5. Becoming. In a Deleuzian conception, becoming is the transformation of life through the refusal of closed structures within which difference can be confined. It is the genesis of structures themselves that becoming reveals. Becoming is not the becoming of A into B, but a state of openness to the movement of pure difference. Working closely with needy adolescents whose backgrounds are anything but trouble-free is challenging work. This was something that was pointed out to me time and again. Talking to older teachers revealed that they had sensed a change in themselves, an opening out, and they had survived because of it. The language toward which they groped was not fully formulated yet. Many of the students at

The City School come from difficult backgrounds, and some seemed to have turned around due to the individual attention of members of the staff. But these slopes of becoming, to speak metaphorically, have steep gradients with considerable uncertainties and variations in relations. For new teachers, the situation is stressful and sometimes affectively draining, especially when it is also accompanied by what they recognize as student disinterest and apathy. In the fairly extensive literature on teacher burnout, there is considerable evidence for believing that beginning teachers are particularly prone to being severely affected in this manner (Weisberg and Sagie, 1999).

The data show a range of coping behaviors. One teacher tended to engage students in extended trivial conversations that led nowhere, another created a strict classroom atmosphere and acknowledged that he was "becoming just the teacher I never wanted to be" (Field Notes 04/08/02). And a third teacher complained of being continually depressed. Typically, mainstream literature talks of "coping strategies" to deal with emotional stress (Abel and Sewell, 1999). But as Byrne (1998) points out, these approaches, instead of opening out, tend to restrict the pedagogical choices available. Our approach to stress and affect will be radically different. It will bypass the humanist route of placing a subject behind feelings or emotions. Instead, it will posit the subject as a construction of intensities or affects. Once situated on this plane of thinking, affects can be reassembled and connected to other intensities.

The Deleuzian praxis I construct in chapter 4 makes available to teachers a mode of becoming in terms of production of signs, or semioticization of the pedagogical encounter, whereby signs, affects, and percepts come together to "release a powerful nonorganic life that escapes the strata, cuts across assemblages, and draws an abstract line of nomad art."(Deleuze and Guattari, 1987, 507). It is art, for it is a fashioning of new alliances and assemblages. It is nomadic, because it is the escaping of the strata that we have encountered before, and that constantly exceeds all confining structures. This line of pure acceleration is therefore a "line of nomad art." As it escapes the strata, it creates new forms and plateaus of intensities or becomings tangentially. By staying on this line of becoming, we develop the potential to counter the problem of stress, which, in a Deleuzian conception, is a passivity. To put it differently, this is the line of active affect.

Conclusion

I do not claim that The City School functioned consciously or unconsciously according to a Deleuzian cartography, nor that it was a nomadic terrain in any extensive sense. The thing I want to suggest is that there were flashes and glimmers of nomadic possibilities in the interstices of the loosened structure, which could have been taken advantage of were the situation and the actors conceptually primed for it. That is to say, the nomadic possibilities could have been actualized in a more significant manner if, into the existing plane of relations, it were possible to introduce the concepts I have been discussing, to make a difference which would then amplify to produce new relations. For these thoughts could perform what Deleuze might call "flection," or a sudden movement of deterritorialization, rather than reflection, which is reproduction.

Further, it is vital to connect up the existing irregular spaces, for example, those that are generated when the experiences from the field enter the classroom, into webs and plateaus through a constant attention to intensity, intricacy, and sensibility infiltrating from the outside, so that by means of such recuperation, the potentialities would intensify, and more creative possibilities could be generated. To put it in the language of systems theory, these intensities can attain an *autopoiesis* or self-generation by means of the existing murmurs that become a "foreign language" through experimentation of the kind I suggest here. In Deleuzian terms, a *plane of composition* can be constructed by means of the concept which, born of necessity, harbors its own forces of becoming, amplifying the existing differential relations (Deleuze and Guattari, 1994). In other words, struggling to be different but still caught in the grip of an older semantics—the signifier regimes that are based on recuperating youthful energies within the matrix of identity, and that cannot enter the irregular spaces—the existing relations in the school needed a different *language of self-description* that would take it to an autopoietic or self-generative plane through amplification.

Part of the goal here is to develop that language from within the concepts we have been discussing; rather than a hermeneutic decoding of the patterns that existed in the school, I "sniff out" the possible openings and in the pages that follow, deterritorialize them further by embedding them in a Deleuzian process of differential becoming. Fortunately for us, Deleuze, together with his coauthor

Guattari, offers a new semiology and a semantics with which each of us can construct our minor or second language within language, a "language of stammering," as Deleuze would say. This language is not about signification and meaning, but about oscillation and resonance with the mass of other becomings.

To summarize then, the effort in this chapter has been to introduce teachers' voices alongside some details about the structure of the school and its curriculum. It is the map under construction or rather a mosaic of smaller maps—superimpositions that allow us to glimpse, from time to time, the not-fully-articulated possibilities of the school, and the directions in which the relations need to move. Second, in the interstices I have inserted Deleuzian reconstellations that do two things: first, they link the data to our framework, and second, they allow us to think in terms of new possibilities of praxis. In order to facilitate the discussion, I have selected some analytical categories that are nothing but certain key spatial qualities of Deleuzian nomadic space. These categories are not hard-edged, but are mere gradients along which to extend the work of theorizing the different aspects of the pedagogic encounters in the school. They capture some important and recurring themes about the nature of spatial relations, and give us a frame for considering some of the difficulties that the novice teachers faced in encountering irregular spaces.

In the following chapter, I will introduce more data from the site and continue the work of analysis that open up the possibilities toward a nomadic topos. This will take the work of mapping one step further. The map of a nomadic topos is unlike any other map; it is at once map and territory. It is nonrepresentational, which is to say, it does not represent but makes connections and projects new lines of flight. Each concept in the map is also a living circuit of becoming, rather than a dead icon. It is a *becoming*-map—therefore, one cannot read this map with the idea of a referent; one can only experiment with it, insert oneself into the making of it even as one constructs it. This is possible because it is a map of intensities, of transformations. In other words, the nomadic map is as much a map of the cartographer herself as it is of the geology of the terrain. Like a normal map, this nomadic cartography has two coordinates: latitude and longitude. But latitude here is the potential for change or degrees of freedom, and longitude is the relations of movement and rest. In other words, bodies and percepts come to be and are related through their differential movements and their potential for transformation. These are coordinates of becoming, and are implicated in the immanent plane whence entities, events, and individuations arise. The interweaving of data and concept that is attempted here is mainly to open as many doors as possible onto this nomadic terrain and experiment with the working of this map even as we produce it, adding small bits at a time.

Chapter 3

Changing the Image of Thought

If thought really yielded to the object, if its attention were on the object, not on its category, the objects would start talking under the lingering eye.
——Theodor Adorno, *Negative Dialectics*

In his well-known ethnographic account titled "Adequate Schools and Inadequate Education: The Life History of a Sneaky Kid," Harry Wolcott (1994) makes the important observation that adequate schools do not necessarily lead to an adequate education. Increasingly, there are youth who, while not averse to learning as the "sneaky kid" testifies, find schools to be impossibly circumscribed spaces, and consequently for them there is no alternative but to drift. Listening and observing at The City School, I find ample confirmation of the above statement in the accounts that I hear, not only from students who had dropped out from regular schools, but among staff as well.

In organizing itself along different lines, The City School in some ways appears to have made an attempt to address some of these issues that Wolcott raises, not only in being more than just an "adequate" school, but in extending schooling in important ways to other areas of social experience. But there is not yet a plane of composition or a "style," as Deleuze would say, that would hold the different pieces or connect the different plateaus or blocks of intensities in an adequately theorized and generative way. By making central to its focus issues of relationship and connectedness, the school makes a serious attempt at constructing conditions of possibility for urban youth to stay connected to education, and makes openings so as to enable them to continue to learn in nonconventional ways. Although there is some literature on service learning, these attempts at innovation remain undertheorized, especially in the context of the genesis and becoming of new teachers.

In this chapter I will discuss two things by means of data and theory: First, we need a different kind of conceptualization of schooling, an epistemological and ontological shift, in order to appreciate the somewhat open, leaky, and indeterminate spaces that can better accommodate "border" youth who cannot fit into mainstream schools. Even within The City School, these spaces remain not fully articulated and not communicating with one another effectively so as to set up a resonance or a synergistic effect that can take the movement beyond itself. I will use Deleuzian concepts to theorize these spaces of indefinitude, or differential formations, that will allow us to remain close to their conditions of emergence. We will produce by means of such an analytic, an intensive composite that can facilitate our work of seeking, or even more, entering praxis. The consequences go well beyond the context of the particular site, not by the attempt to generalize, which carries the flavor of essentialization, but by creating the conditions that can realize the importance of singularities or unique constellations of forces and historio-geographies of intensity.

Second, I will suggest that the difficulties novice teachers face on entering such an environment, where there is less reliance on the conventional curriculum, and a significant absence as well of appeals to conventional authority for structure and discipline, are, to a large extent, the result of certain unexamined conceptual conventions that dominate perception that result in turning away from creative openings and toward a self-imposed containment in representational space. This part of the exploration will be carried out as a relay of theory between points of practice, and practice acting as relays between theoretical points in a nondialectical, multiplicitous manner.

By means of this strategy, we will place under examination the very commonplaces and categories on which the experience called "school" is built. Examining the primary drives of seeking order in the classroom, perceiving learning as coincident with what takes place within its boundaries, and looking for certainty in the curricular process contrast with the possibility that learning might take place in surprising, nonlocalizable, and in-between spaces, through connections rather than in specific significations, and in ways that are uncertain and sometimes inarticulable.

We will see how pedagogical opportunities are missed in this setup by holding on to the mainstream or conventional positions on learning and curriculum, and also demonstrate the differential spaces and possibilities in the school. This is based on what I learned from the conversations and observations at the school, which showed that the thing that seemed most important to these students was a sense of belonging, as well as deeper communication with adults, both of which often lie beyond the circumscribed roles of teachers in regular settings. This is not to claim that mainstream schooling is monolithic or homogeneous, but to point out that the overall emphasis that arranges education in a techno-bureaucratic space missed the boat, so to speak, where these urban youth were concerned. This view is corroborated by JS, a novice teacher, who tells me: "I come from a minority community, and went to school in the city. The large public schools did nothing for me…I came close to dropping out, and there are many like me. That is why I came to teaching, to do something different." (Field Notes 04/12/02) The system forced JS to occupy spaces where he was not affirmed, and did not give credence to his own *Lebenswelt* and sensibilities. This is the plight of many urban adolescents who have been *standardized out* of the system, and find their way to the innovative school.

In this connection, Giroux (2000) points out that

> the dominant features of public schooling are characterized by a modernist project that has increasingly come to rely upon instrumental reason and the standardization of curricula. (177)

This centered curricula, Giroux further observes, that is devoted to the rule of a certain narrow kind of disjointed "reason," and in which affects and emotions mostly find no place except to pathologize youth, is a heavily "coded cultural legacy…that privileges the histories, experiences, and cultural capital of largely white, middle-class students" (178). In Deleuzian language, these are spaces governed by "strata," and captured by "molar" or majoritarian politics. We have to find, instead, fissures and lines of escape from molar into "molecular" becomings within curriculum, that is, remappings on a transformational matrix of minoritarian politics.[1]

In a school that attempts to serve marginalized youth, teachers need not merely a separate set of skills, but new lenses through which to rethink curriculum as a whole. It is therefore an important move to help teachers equip themselves with the necessary theoretical tools and concepts with which to remap what is going on, and gain a fresh perspective on things; a perspective that helps to move away from the old habits of thought, and abandon worn-out spaces. And for this purpose, we turn to Deleuze, who attempts what may be called a perspectival reversal of Platonism in order to form a new sense of a geography of intensities born of the irregularities of thought. To reiterate, it is not in regularized spaces, but from the *irregularities,* that a new thought is born. Therefore, the added value of seeing the processes through a Deleuzian lens is that it will allow teachers to see in a positive light the very slippages, affects, and other "unruly" curricular experiences that tend to embarrass technocratic rationality, and look at these as new possibilities for curriculum development.

Deleuze is also an artist of unfinished geometries, of "what might yet happen," and ceaselessly constructs in order to free life forces from being captive in regulated spaces or previously staked-out ground. In this chapter, I frequently use the Deleuzian notion of the "rhizome" for drawing out the possibilities of multiple connections, and emergent, as opposed to reified, relations between the student, the curriculum, and the context. The rhizome moves and grows in unpredictable ways and never attains a fixed and final form. I do not claim that the school was already functioning with a Deleuzian perspective; rather that the existing conditions would be better served or its potentialities actualized, if such a perspective were to be deliberately introduced in the thinking of the place. Small changes amplified through feedback would, by conceptually realigning the discourse, create conditions for new oscillations or resonances to arise. Also I claim that, in communicating with the new teachers about the alternative possibilities of the school, such a theoretical perspective would be invaluable.

As we saw in the previous chapter, the fluidity and the multiplicity of roles, and the necessity of slipping in and out of different functional and perceptive areas is disturbing and unsettling for those who have been used to the security of more circumscribed roles. L.S., whom we have met before, and I continue our conversation:

> K.R.: It seems to me from what you have said until now that you are referring to more than just a list of things or skills that is needed. You seem to be suggesting that there's something else operating that one needs to get acquainted with. Can you comment?
>
> L.S.: Well, it is a sort of culture. I mean in the regular schools you did things the way…there were lots of guidelines and the expectations were clear. Here, it is like it comes out of the culture of the place. Things are not as explicit.
>
> K.R.: Does that make it problematic?
>
> L.S.: I am not always sure what the students are learning. So things do seem more chaotic. (Interview with L.S. No.2)

Let us recall the issue of decentered authority as an aspect of "smoothness" from the analytical structure laid out in the previous chapter. L.S. gives us a good example of the kinds of certainty many teachers look for in their practice, which, in the language of the present analysis, is a search for a supplementary dimension since only an external relation can guarantee certainty. That supplemental dimension could be the formal structure of schooling, a standardized curriculum, the relations of power and hierarchy, or simply a kind of habitus (Bourdieu, 1990) that structures pedagogical response. But in each case, it is a movement away from the performative present, from the immanence of action. Supplementarity thus may be opposed to spontaneity. L.S., as the above conversation illustrates, wants order in the form of rules and definite expectations. She is also looking to be trained in the correct way to do things. She uses the term "culture" to mark a difference, of not being at ease in a space that is unfamiliar. L.S. wants to be sure of "what the students are learning," perhaps in clear quantifiable terms. But research has shown that what students learn is often unpredictable and uncertain, and depends less on predetermined activity than on the goings-on at various levels in a given context at a given time (Davis et al., 2000, 4–12). Learning thus occurs or emerges at the intersection of complex factors that cannot be fully controlled. But the need for surety and certainty is so ingrained that we rarely stop to question it. Hartley (1997) observes:

The school is a monument to modernity. Virtually everything is arranged rationally, including space, time, curriculum, assessment and discipline. Children are classified according to a range of criteria. Rules regulate us. There are set procedures [for everything]....Schools are places where reason prevails over emotions" (125).

It is probably going too far to say that in schools "reason prevails over emotion," for I am not sure how many of us would agree that schools are always reasonable places, although they seemingly carry out the functions of a certain structure, discarding in the process the breadth of sensation. But given that achievement of instrumental order is of the highest priority, it is not surprising that LS feels uncertain in her role at The City School, whose working represents what Hartley calls a "lapse" that is "too unwieldy for our tidy-minded modern ways" (125). The unwieldiness comes from an entangled, multiplicitous, and divergent space in which things refuse to fall into neat categories. The entangled character of curricular relations in the school leads me to posit the concept of multiplicities—a key Deleuzian term. Every event or entity, including ourselves, is a multiplicity, or rather, multiplicities. Beneath the apparent unity or coherence of an entity, or an event, lie fields of flux and multiple layers of unformed or not-fully-formed elemental states. Through selective processes, there arise out of these fields temporary assemblages of elements, composites that follow abstract lines of development and organization, through what may be called a "connective synthesis."[2] All phenomena thus are multiplicities on a plane of continual variation.

Thinking in terms of multiplicities becomes important, and gains praxial power when we realize that each abstract line of potentiality or combinations of sense-matter-thought that enters into a composite also has an escape, a mutational possibility not necessarily coincident with inverse transformations. That is to say, although events or entities are born of capture producing the perception of phenomena, there are also exits or escapes from these molar categories. Multiplicities can be rearranged, disassembled, and reassembled to form new assemblages. This means that thought and affect can be transformed and extended in previously unthought-of ways by taking into account sensations and intensities that were previously excluded. For teachers operating in bleak urban landscapes that seem to offer few breaks, and charged with the task of engaging students who seem to have limited options within modernist categories and assumptions, operationalizing a Deleuzian cartography loosens the boundaries within which thought can think. Formerly stratified material suddenly become available for opening out the curriculum. The molecularization of previously stratified material gives a fleeting glimpse of a deterritorialized moment.

The phenomenon of operational multiplicity can emerge in multiple ways. When students' views and life experiences are affirmed, a class of individuals can be suddenly transformed into a synergistic extension with connectivities proliferating in many directions. Another name for operational multiplicities used by Deleuze is the rhizome. Rhizomes are contrasted to trees or arborescent systems; whereas trees are vertically ordered, rhizomes tend to be nonhieratic, laterally connected multiplicities that do not feature linear development. Like tubers and mosses, they grow laterally and entangled, and like knowledge, they are messy; any point on a rhizome can be connected to any other point, making such a structure open and dependent on emergent relations. Rhizomes can be interrupted at any point only to start up again, proliferating lines of flight that sprout contingently, not according to fixed pathways. They thrive in irregular and in-between spaces, and have no specific starting or ending point; they are always in the middle, in transition, on the verge of becoming something else. Rhizomes are structures of intensity.

As I observed the workings of the school, it seemed to me that the concept of the rhizome is particularly suitable for theorizing the tendencies and potentialities of the narrative and descriptive spaces of The City School. With the possibility of organizing the curriculum in several ways, of initiating new ways of evaluation, as well as in its connection to the field, a rhizomatic description seemed to be a fruitful way of conceptualizing the situation, one that would allow teachers to make new connections. Experimenting on ourselves as rhizomes or collectivities that are laterally connected gives us room to challenge the inner authority of our selective procedures and boundary constructs that exclude other ways of looking at schooling than the representational. The rhizome is at the same time an analytical tool and a *becoming* that can help in constructing new spaces for teaching and learning. As a tool of analysis, it helps us to see the possibilities and connections in a non-Cartesian way, that is, in nonbinary modes of thinking. As a way of becoming, it allows us to conceive of linking our collectivities to other assemblages for acting upon, say, the curriculum, embodying our sensibilities to extend it in unaccustomed directions. Besides, for Deleuze, concepts like the rhizome are really vectors that have a force and direction of their own, extending the possibilities in the synaptic structures of the brain itself. In other words, thinking in this way changes the very architecture of the brain.

Introducing this vital Deleuzian notion, I suggest that the school has in it potential rhizoid spaces. I watch a minor student "revolt." The students insist that the name of the school be changed. The actual name, which obviously cannot be revealed here, is found to evoke certain associations that are unacceptable to many of them. After several discussions there is a confrontation with the staff over this, and a referendum is proposed. Staff and students agree to do a survey on possible alternatives and let it go to the ballot. The importance of this event lay not in the inversion of power relationships but in the animation and passion it generated. Curriculum can be seen to be the embodied intensities that develop when things close to the students are allowed to occur. For these reasons one might say that a rhizomatic possibility exists in the school. Therefore, the example cited above must not be confused with student empowerment. The rhizome grows from within, making the necessary connections in a system environment coupling, whereas the notion of empowerment invokes an external empowering agent. In the above instance, the forces emerged more from the way in which students were related to the school than from any conscious effort to empower.

Deleuze and Guattari (1987) contrast the open structure of the rhizome that can grow offshoots in any direction, to the hierarchical structure of the tree or "arborescent" systems that are linear. Trees do not grow roots in the foliage, nor can they grow leaves among the root system. They are inflexible, and bound by the rules of stratification:

> Strata are Layers, Belts. They consist of giving form to matters, of imprisoning intensities or locking singularities into molar aggregates. Strata are acts of capture, they are like black holes striving

to capture whatever comes within their reach. (40)

Strata are bands produced by thickening; they generate gravitational fields, fields of determinate spaces like techno-managerial ones that provide a sense of certainty and security. To seek certainty in the context of learning is to inhabit striated space; that is, to operate in determined territories that resist border crossings, and therefore cut communication lines stretching across boundaries. Open borders are terrains of uncertainty and are the very conditions of the possibility of learning—a fresh movement in thought. The growth of the rhizome in unpredictable ways and its self-description can provide learning with a cross-fertilization between widely separated lateral spaces that promote a dramatization of knowledge. As discussed below, the open borders of learning attempted by the LEAPs, which act as an interface between the activities at the placements and school-based learning, allow for a level of indeterminacy and creative uncertainty to disturb the strata. They open up the interstices, the sewn-up structure of rigid domains.

Curriculum as Rhizome
The LEAPs that trouble most of the novice teachers are as much a creative effort as a procedural one. There is no one way of doing the LEAPs, since placements change all the time, new ones are added, and some old ones are dropped. Additionally, teachers have to design the LEAPs according to the project the student is working on at the placements; it cannot be generic. For example, at a placement in the Legal Action Council, a student may either work on a project that is based in history or in citizenship studies. The teacher must create a LEAP that is congruent with the project, and the disciplinary credit must be granted accordingly. Further, students' requirements are different, and each configuration is required to dovetail with in-house classes that lead to the necessary credits for graduation. In this way, curriculum appears more like a rhizoid structure, concerned with building connections. *Thinking* the rhizome or entering a rhizomatic mode allows us to conceive of more connections, not because the rhizome is an effective model or a metaphor—that is, it is not a mode of organizing sensibilities from which we break into new orders of thought—but because it releases us from the false bondage of linear relationships, and allows us, even if momentarily, to realize our

multiplicities, that which is always already (to use a Heideggerian phrase). In other words, we *live* the rhizome or the rhizome lives in us, and we ask what constructs we want and what determinations and intensities we are prepared to countenance.

The curriculum seen more like a rhizome, that is, in terms of connectivities and relationalities rather than as a preformed and pre-given structure, has many other advantages. It foregrounds precisely those aspects of exchange that are filtered out in the regular curriculum processes, affirming intensities that are unaccounted for within mainstream discourses. As Deleuze points out, rhizomes are offshoots, not sowings; irregular growths, not deliberate plantings. A rhizomatic conception allows affective investments and existential narratives to enter the learning environment obliquely and powerfully, in irregular ways, opportunities not provided for by the official curriculum, connecting the classroom with the lived realities of the social actors in the school. In other words, every movement, gesture, autobiographical event, and accidental phenomenon can become a learning opportunity, including those that are considered disruptive behavior. The mimic, the bully, and the class clown become contributors to the curriculum once the archive of presuppositions that inform those actions are reconnected to the learning process. L.S.'s concerns about what the students are learning are mostly to do with learning on the visible and conscious level. But as Davis et al. (2000) point out, learning at the conscious level is only a small fragment of learning that goes on at other levels, and too much focus on the conscious aspect can lead to a starvation of the senses. As we see later on, there is important learning going on in nonregulated spaces, learning that is important for the lives of these young people.

Coming from a way of doing things that is firmly "territorialized," or set in the practice of containment, as well as predetermined in terms of the intended effects, the activities at the school seem "chaotic" to L.S.; but she acknowledges that seeing the various activities as disparate and isolated from one another is not helpful either. Instead, as she noted earlier, it all seemed to come out of a certain "culture." This culture is what we might call a "practice of the contingent," the exercise of a not-fully-determined space which is an important tool for survival for a school catering to uncertain urban conditions.

But contingency is seen "as an enemy" of the governmentalized social order (Bauman 1992). Giroux (2000) observes:

> Rather than accepting the modernist assumption[s]…it makes more sense in the present historical moment to educate students to theorize differently about the meaning of work in a post-modern world. Indeterminacy rather than order should become the guiding principle of a pedagogy in which multiple views, possibilities, and differences are opened up as part of an effort to read the future contingently. (179)

Partly, the necessity for understanding the nature of contingency arises from the changed global conditions related to work, markets, media, and identities that require new forms of literacy on the part of the teacher as well as the student, since both have to face these radically changed postindustrial conditions in which the character of the economy, culture, and knowledge have become uncertain. I do not mean to suggest here that schools ought to change in order to fit in with the emergent world order and help to normalize it, but that curriculum must take advantage of fissures that arise in times of acute change, and open up complex, indeterminate regions that are "not-fully-formed" elements but patches of intensities and connections. The following is an example of the predicament teachers face in this changing and problematic space:

> T.G.: Take S, she is currently undergoing training for six weeks and is out of school. This is part of the W2 requirements. The law now requires that she get training in order to qualify for welfare; she is a teenage mom and wants to complete school. However, by the time she completes training, she will turn 18 and so legally she can be asked to work full time. That effectively puts her out of school and she can kiss graduation goodbye. We here have decided not to let that happen. So she is taking independent studies with us and that will give her the few required credits she needs to graduate. One of our teachers goes to visit her regularly to check up on how she is doing. She is a diligent student and will graduate but we have to find ways and means and come up with creative solutions to these conditions that kids face. They are at the intersection of work, the law, poverty and needing to

graduate. (Interview with T.G. No.1)

Here is an instance of the problem of being captured in strata. As T.G. relates it, there is a gap between what the students need and what bureaucratized education provides, a gap between schooling and education. Nancy Lesko (1995) has identified such mixed needs that policy is unable to come to terms with as "leaky needs" (199). There is a necessity for teachers to find creative solutions to meet such leaky needs and find the resources to be able to do so. Often, it is the flexibility and the mutual understanding that the teachers have developed between themselves that provide the ground for this additional "respond-ability." But a more important analytical moment is missed if we do not see that this is also the opportunity to form a new composite. The projecting of curriculum onto an Outside makes for a different order of *integration that is based on differentiation.* A lesson in social studies becomes more of a distribution of point intensities in a field that lie beyond the utterances since it is continuously modified and modulated by the intensities of the space surrounding S. That is, it must be worked through the set of implicit presuppositions that forms the context of S, freeing a whole set of minor narratives that lie as murmurs buried in the context. This development of a "minor language" of intensities allows us to escape gridded or state space and enter what, in terms of our Deleuzian categories, I have called smooth space; to recall, it is marked by an open-ended quality, and on its surface one can move from any point to any other point with less hindrance.

This creates a bridgehead for a radical kind of empiricism, a pluralism that indicates, in this particular instance, that innovative circumstances can do more than accommodate S with a lesson in math or social studies at home. An attention to much that is in the in-between spaces that contain molecular intensities needs to be explored. This cannot be fully mapped out in advance, but an awareness of a plane of continuous variation between school and S that changes every moment may be worked on as a curricular opportunity. Let me try and put it differently: One way of seeing this is to look at it as lessons being delivered to a student by a teacher; that is, contacts between molar categories. This is the way we are usually conditioned to look. A different way of looking I am suggesting here is to see this process as distorting a plane of variations, like a sheet of rubber which is the composite field that can be stretched and manipulated to produce different shapes on its surface, somewhat akin to a topological plane. There are no categories here but only currents, flows, and eddies, and the "teacher" brings different gradients of becoming to such irregular spaces. On such a plane, the categories disappear momentarily to produce arrangements or what Deleuze calls *agencements*, a term that closely parallels Foucault's notion of the *dispositif*. The deployment of these intensities necessarily begins from a certain degree of deterritorializing or shedding of strata that makes room for new sensitivities and resonances. And the social studies lesson becomes a study of the socially embedded ways of perception and the escape from it.

From a critique of State space, it is possible to read the above example as a mechanism that does not concern itself with the underlying ideology of W2, but merely ensures that the student falls in line with the State machinery. But the thing to which I point here is the multiplicitous and contingent becomings on the gradient of the plane of curriculum, and the molecular possibilities on that plane; each a possible line of escape from State space. So the confrontation with power is through experimentation that breaks open the molar categories on which power depends, to reveal fluctuating fields. And it is the resonance issuing from the site that alerts me to the latent possibilities of using a Deleuzian framework in order to build micro-circuits of change, small unravelings at a minor level. These timbres suggest the possibility of transformation in the encounter along frequencies not usually considered by teachers in more conventional settings.

The plane of becoming or composition is a key Deleuzian (Deleuze and Guattari, 1987) concept in which incorporeal transformations take place that insinuate us into new arrangements:

> The plane of composition knows nothing of substance and form. It consists of modes of individuation, in relations of speed and slowness between unformed elements, and in compositions of corresponding intensive affects [that tie] together heterogeneous multiplicities of the rhizome type. (507)

Substance and form are useful, but they become obstructive to the process of transformation and becoming when overemphasized, as in the modernist curriculum. We are always in the middle, Deleuze would remind us—the teacher is as much in a larval state as the student, and so is the curriculum. One errs in thinking that any of these are finished products. The plane of composition is rather like a topological space on which one can distort a triangle to produce a square, an octagon, or even a circle. Deleuze offers conceptions of speed and slowness, flows, densities, and transformations that help us to change the image of ourselves in thought, and consequently, open ourselves to the transhuman, unraveling the body's molar organization, exploring different zones of intensity. These variations of "speed," or acceleration, become evident when we continually push against ourselves, against our boundaries and the limits of discourses. There is a movement of continuous transformation rather than any major break. This hydraulic quality allows us to open up boundaries long reified by linguistic habits and cultural normalizations. This is micro-resistance, at the minoritarian level.

In the concept of multiplicities, and the plane of continuous variation in which individuations occur to form different plateaus of intensities, a Deleuzian viewpoint offers a rhizomatics of connectivities that goes beyond the autonomous individual that is emphasized by the moderns. The word individuation as employed here must not be confused with the notion of individuality. Individuation refers to intensities, traits, or attributes that are *pre-individual*, that is, preexist the entity, and continue into other becomings even after the entity has ceased to exist. Thus, an individual is only a loose arrangement of individuations that come together and break up under different statistical processes. The pedagogic implication is that learning takes place in the interstices of these individuations, in the in-between regions, and between bodies and the curriculum, thereby permitting new arrangements. This manner of looking reveals the radical possibilities of new kinds of conjugations unthought-of before that are composed of singularities or unique moments of the world.

Observe below the reactions of LS, who sees the lack of academic rigor and equipment in the school as problematic and is frustrated by her construct of science as a formalistic exercise:

L.S.: Going over to the science museum, what does it achieve? I would not give science credit for it. I'm sure of that.

K.R.: Does it fit in some other way with the rest of the program?
L.S.: Maybe. But it cannot compensate for competency in specific
areas such as science. I don't believe it can.
K.R.: What about making connections in general, would you
consider that as part of science education?
L.S.: You have to be more specific than that. My frustration is
with this lack of specificity, for example with the fact that I find
no science equipment. That's another source of tension for me.
Nothing here to show that the school has been up and running
for the last eight years. (Interview with L.S. No. 2 and follow-up
Conversation)

While from a certain perspective L.S. cannot be faulted for
demanding standard elements of curriculum for her students, she is
also trapped by strict category-oriented thinking; she is concerned
that students are not obtaining the science lab experience at the
museum but she does not consider the possibility of investigating the
whole system of utterances and nondiscursive manipulations or
embodiments that might arise from working at the museum, as a
viable alternative mode of organizing the senses that might in
different ways link up with moments of the world. The consequence
of shutting out the latter is a sense of lack and the persistent feeling of
not recovering adequately what is out there. But consider Varela
(1992) in this context:

> Cognitive science is waking up to the full importance of the
> realization that perception does not consist in the recovery of a
> pre-given world, but rather in the perceptual guidance of action
> in a world that is inseparable from our sensorimotor capacities.
> (17)

Learning, therefore, consists not of recovery or recognition, but what
Varela calls "embodied action." In other words, there is an immense
field of relations waiting to be tapped into once we shed our
restrictive ways of looking. It is to the pedagogic possibilities of
embodied action that L.S. must be invited to open her mind, instead
of being fixated solely upon the recovery of existing knowledge. I
argue that such an approach works better in the urban situation and
moves away from the notion of lack or deficiency. Deleuze points out

that our fixation on deficiency or lack is due to a general Oedipal orientation that prevents our opening up to the forces that lie within the immediate: "In order to harness the active forces that lie embedded within mutant empires of reactivity, [we] must acquire an altered sensibility to deficiency and lack" (Conway, 1997, 82). Therefore, although The City School, through its innovative curriculum, has made attempts to mine the urban context for providing learning opportunities, beginning teachers like L.S. are conceptually underprepared for it.

Consider yet another example of how the allegiance to rigid boundaries brings about frustration in its wake. We see A.D., a teacher new to the innovative setting, and who comes from having previously taught in a more academically oriented school, expressing concern for low academic standards:

> I feel like I am doing nothing here. I feel like I am wasting my time here. The standard is so low and students do not show any interest in learning at all. I am saying to them, ask me questions, I am here for you. There are so few students in the class, so take advantage of this. (Interview with A.D. No.1)

A.D. sees the "low" standard as a problem of the Outside, as an objective thing, and gives it a transcendent meaning beyond the active processes of which he is a part. But where is the "standard," this formal abstraction of the level of ignorance? In terms of our analysis, the "standard" that A.D. refers to requires a supplemental dimension for its conception. To recall the discussion in chapter 2, this supplemental dimension is provided by an act of "overcoding" that codifies or stratifies the emergent into fixed categories of investment. Otherwise, there is only process and the movement of intensity. I suggest that if A.D. is helped to perceive himself as part of the process he is discursively engaged in, that is to say, if he learns to let himself into the plane of composition as a composite being himself, the issue of low standards evaporates. In other words, the supplemental dimension collapses, and the teaching moments appear as the molar categories come apart.

Further, in terms of pedagogy, A.D.'s "ask me questions" approach is a displacement of burden within reified categories, and a symptom of the traditional role of teacher as repository of knowledge. Britzman (1986) has observed:

> The view of the teacher as expert also tends to reinforce the image of teacher as *autonomous* individual. As a possession, knowledge also implies *territorial* rights, which become naturalized by the compartmentalization of curriculum. The cultural myth of teachers as experts, then, contributes to the reification of both knowledge and the knower. (450–51) (emphasis added)

Throughout our discussion, I have questioned in various ways the notion of autonomy. I have inserted the pedagogical relation in the plane of composition and asked that we consider the existence of the various elements on this plane as existing only in reciprocal presupposition. In other words, I have asked that we consider abandoning the molar categories, and instead, treat the learning encounter as an event that can arise only in between. The refrain "I am the teacher, ask me" is precisely a negation of this principle of mutual determination that results in a boundary problem and that needs to be deterritorialized. In my own experience in urban schools, the "ask me" approach rarely works. For teaching and learning are much more furtive and surreptitious acts than is often acknowledged, and in the representational space of the formal curriculum furtive moves appear disingenuous and are routinely suppressed through intricate disciplinary measures, indirect discourses, and systems of reward and punishment.

Micropolitics of Rhizoid Space

Continuing our conversation, A.D. is also irritated by what he sees as an unsupportive atmosphere. It is exacerbated by different perceptions of what the role of the teacher is here:

> A.D.: This is the most hostile environment that I have come across in all my years of teaching.
> K.R.: Can you elaborate on that a little bit?
> A.D.: They don't do any orientation here at all. And yet it is supposed to be different. New people are left to find out things themselves.
> K.R.: Are there other reasons why you feel that this place is

hostile?

A.D.: Yes, there are other reasons. It's hard to put your finger on them. The atmosphere of the place is part of it. Some people here like to think of themselves as really big and go about shouting "We built this school"; So what? They think that they are the only ones doing the work. R.S. [referring to another teacher] told some visitors that I watch TV! Yes, I watch the news when I finish teaching. I am not disturbing anyone and what else do I do when I finish teaching? (Interview with A.D. No.1)

R.S., an older teacher, responds to A.D.'s comments underlining the tensions that run among the staff, and the differences in perceptions between new teachers and older members as to the extent of responsibilities :

One day he said—"Well, it is 2:00 pm and I am going to get a haircut"! Sorry, if you are here and you have no teaching to do then you should go out and start cultivating some resources. That is why he was hired. (Interview with R.S. No.1)

Although a different sort of problem, I deliberately include this here as a part of the tensions around curricular issues and therefore worth discussing. While it is part of the district teachers' union, The City School has relied more on internal negotiations to determine how the unconventional nature of its curricular demands could be met by the group. The older staff insist that they do not wish to impose their vision on newcomers, but as Cherryholmes (1988) has observed, the search for a negotiated settlement "cannot proceed without normative commitments and power arrangements" (91). Here we have a double bind: the senior staff not wanting to exercise authority but wanting newcomers to "voluntarily" see the needs of the place. I suggest that a way out of this double bind can be found in Deleuzian pragmatics, and for that it will be necessary for us to understand the important Deleuzian (1990) notion of disjunctive synthesis.

For Deleuze, divergence is not a principle of exclusion, nor is disjunction a means of separation. Rather, disjunction and divergence are a means of communication. In order to explain this, let us consider the two opposing series—the older teachers' views versus the new staff's attitudes. Seen in a Deleuzian light, we will find that the successive terms of the opposition do not coincide. That is to say, although there is a disjunction above, each series is necessarily heterogeneous and presents elements that are full of "holes." Each successive term in any series opens itself up to "the infinity of predicates through which it passes," and "the communication of events replaces the exclusion of predicates." This infinitely holed surface that is like a sieve cannot provide absolute opposition, which requires identity, and hence, what appeared as hard-edged predicates turn out to be events or processes or becomings. This is what makes it possible to bring about communication between the two series since they now exist in reciprocal presupposition, and not as self-enclosed elements of opposition:

> The synthetic disjunction consists of the erection of a paradoxical instance, an aleatory point with two uneven faces,which traverses the divergent series as divergent and causes them to resonate through their distance and in their distance. (Deleuze, 1990b, 174)

Communication happens through a "resonance of disparates"; that is, by giving up the illusion that the two series are made up of "solid" and independent contraries, we become aware not of the identity of contraries but of resonances. What this implies is that oppositional terms in both series when investigated turn out to be heterogeneous, and as events that depend upon context rather than preexist as fixed predicates. This takes us into a zone of the "impersonal and pre-individual singularities" (175). To put it differently, it is a withdrawal from reified structures of thought-affect to more fluid states. Deleuze (1995) writes,

> There's nothing transcendent, no Unity, Subject, Reason; there are only processes. These processes are at work in concrete multiplicities. It's multiplicities that fill the field of immanence. [It] has to be constructed... any given multiplicity is like one area of the plane....[U]nifications often amount to an impasse or closing off that prevents the multiplicity's growth. (145–46)

Processes have no subject; for example, "it's raining"; this has been known since the days of Heraclitus. Similarly, pleasure and pain do not happen to subjects, rather, their molecular oscillations give rise to the idea of the subject or a center of perception. Further, for Deleuze, these processes are becomings or "nonsubjective individuations" that arise out of a million micro-contractions or percepts, and can enter into other becomings to form a plane of immanence, or patchwork productions. In this new image of ourselves as process or patchwork, we can break out of the double bind by entering a different level of description than the one we are familiar with.

Curriculum, Lack and Resistance

Immanence affirms life, eschewing the notion of lack. Deleuze helps us to change the image of ourselves, moving from entities that lack something or other when measured against preexisting models, to processes and composites, currents and intensities that are under production. But modernist education has increasingly brought a culture of deficiency, and along with that a sense of alienation among youth. Concerned about the despair and dislocation in contemporary youth, and the consequent ebbing away of "ethical discrimination," Giroux (2000) has contended that, "The challenge for critical educators is to question how a transformative pedagogy might be employed [for] appropriating some of [postmodernism's] more radical aspects" (181). One of these radical aspects is the rethinking of lack, which is a vestigial Oedipal reaction recuperated within Capitalism that serves to control and subjugate.

Reading Giroux along with Massumi's (1992) commentary on Deleuze, one major concern that needs careful attention is the "consumer/commodity axis of the capitalist relation" that increasingly allows participation in the life of the world only as consumers, and the manner in which this positions youth (133). This is certainly an example of control through lack. Massumi contends that although the body's realm of possibility has expanded infinitely, the transformational potential is still, for the most part, subordinated to the axiomatics of capitalist relations. In order to release transformative potentialities from the grip of existing power relations, we have to realize and embrace our collectivities that present an avenue for escaping the consumer/commodity relation.

And this becomes possible when we begin to think in terms of production, specifically the production of *affect:* "For affect is not a personal feeling, nor is it a characteristic; it is the effectuation of a power of the pack that throws the [constituted] self into upheaval and makes it reel," and when we cross over into our multiplicities, into becomings that release active passions, we become "sorcerers" (Deleuze and Guattari, 1987, 240–41). The sorcerer goes to the a-signifying semiotic and extracts therefrom the world of affect and singularities.³ Sorcery is simply another name for a *becoming other* by connecting up to new affects. Thus initiated, we turn the tables on lack, and move from passive consumerism to active production. Desire, or active passion, is the matrix of production, and contains the possibility of taking us beyond our molar subjectivities that are trapped within the axiomatics of Capital. Also, unlike psychoanalytic space where desire is a lack, here it becomes the very field of production; this redescription is powerful and affirming, and is able to replace lack by a proliferation of possibilities, especially in the pedagogic encounter.

But what does this mean in concrete terms for teachers? It means that as we destratify through the internalization of a different cartography that is being presented here, minuscule cracks appear in the façade of reality that is of pure breach. This allows the entity-series to move beyond itself. It takes us momentarily beyond crystallizations, and there are new individuations within curriculum as a result, new arrangements that are more open, more generative and affirmative. For instance, it can open us toward affirming the unknown which, in a sense, is pure difference:

> [The] group of an equation does not characterize at a given moment what we know about its roots, but the objectivity of what we do not know about them. Conversely, this non-knowledge is no longer a negative or an insufficiency but…something *to be learnt* which corresponds to a fundamental dimension of the object. The whole pedagogical relation is transformed…[and] many other things along with it, including knowledge and sufficient reason. (Deleuze, 1994, 180)

Although Deleuze writes this using the context of the theory of groups that revolutionized mathematics, and it is characteristic of his work to rely on mathematics to clarify his ontology, the argument easily lends itself to our discussion here. The non-knowledge *transforms* the "whole pedagogical relation." In other words, we see the affirmative character of that which is beyond conscious knowledge that can change our understanding of knowledge and the nature of reason. This does not refer to a sea of suppressed unconscious activity, but rather to a becoming or an emergence, a virtual dimension beyond the actual. With this displacement or decentering comes a wholly new way of relating to knowledge and reason. Although we have come a little way in opening a discussion about the praxeological implications, we have some more work to do before we can construct more of this particular map.

Thus far, we have seen how The City School offers new challenges and reveals irregular learning spaces that often result in difficulties for new teachers when they are unable to appeal to the authority of conventional assumptions about teaching and learning. I have suggested that a Deleuzian lens is useful for teachers not only to consider what is going on in those fissures but that such a perspective helps us to loosen the boundaries and assumptions about the identities or strata in which we are often "locked." This is important, for how we think is closely tied to our notion of who we are. Such a praxis of "destratification" in the way of an apprenticeship of the sign is offered in the following chapter. In the rest of this chapter I will explore the differential spaces that arise in the school that further shed light on how a Deleuzian pragmatics might contribute to teacher becoming. Our attempt will be to find ways to make the two series—teacher and school—resonate in positive ways.

Difference and Repetition

The present is always problematic and multiple, not only because it is the ground for a colossal struggle between different pasts and different lenses, but also because it is a contest between different futures and different desires. It is this present as a passage I have to contend with in my relationship to the school, for as a researcher I am in that eternal present. Every time I walk into The City School, the first thing I notice about the atmosphere is a certain gruff security. Students look me in the eye, and some nod or smile, but there is also ambiguity that is also a disjunctive synthesis of the qualitative differences that produce those responses. What is this present if not a difference, a distinction that cannot be put into a preexisting mold in order to make sense? What the school has not eliminated is a certain productive sense of indeterminacy that comes partly out of the fact that these students have not been made faceless, and partly because they spend a lot of their time in placements, and bring those qualitatively different experiences with them into the school everyday, through the day.

Consequently, there seems to be a clearing here, a differential space in which, besides the repetitious formal curriculum, "issues of allegiance, commitment, destruction, trauma, and community can be taken seriously" (Britzman and Dippo, 2000, 36). In other words, there is space to consider issues that often tend to get censored or elided or reduced by repetition into facile vocabulary and unproblematized assumptions. One teacher, C.M., tells me that she has been helping some of the teenage single mothers with day care issues and other kinds of support that are key to their remaining in school. C.M. denies that this is out of a sense of charity, but instead says "it is a building of something in myself" (Field Notes 04/12/02). In Deleuzian terms, it is a *becoming-other* she experiences, that is, a differential relation, too easily passed over as a subjective feeling.

It will be useful to pause here and delve briefly into Deleuzian ontology, especially his differential theory of production:

A particular object is the result of the particular rule of its production or the mode of its differential, and the relations between different objects result from the relations between their differentials.   (Salomon Maïmon cited in Deleuze, 1994, 174)

In other words, objects are in reciprocal determination through the relations between their differentials. I know red from green not because of any intrinsic qualitative property that distinguishes them, but because the two sets of vibrations—one made up of the rods and cones of my eye and the other of the surface interactions of the object—resonate on certain frequencies. There is a synthesis of differences or a disjunctive synthesis. Now, what consequences might this have for us, or how does it help us to know about reciprocal determination at that level? I suggest that systematically employed, these concepts might unleash in us fresh oscillations by making apparent the groundlessness that surrounds us, making us less oriented toward the static and more interested in the dynamic relationalities of formations. Such conceptual awareness alters our predispositions. Pedagogically this is powerful, since it opens a door onto a more open plane or what I have referred to as the "nomadic."

Moreover, Deleuze continues, "the differential is indeed pure power, just as the differential relation is a pure element of potentiality" (175). The differential or pure difference is an undetermined quantity: The biologist and anthropologist Gregory Bateson (1991) pointed out that the difference between the chalk and the board is neither in the chalk, nor in the board, nor in the space between the two, and therefore it escapes determination. This is precisely why the differential is able to carry out the determinations that we ask of it such as the production of objects of perception. This is also why it is "pure power," carrying the power of determination. On the other hand, the differential relation is a potential since it is the possibility of any two series resonating with each other. The sum of all these potentialities is what Deleuze refers to as the *virtual*. All production is thus the actualization of the virtual. Before continuing, I must make it clear that the virtual must not be confused with popular terms like "virtual reality" that are associated with simulations produced by means of computer technology and so-called cyberspace. The latter is no more virtual than the hardware itself is.

The pedagogical consequence of this is significant as is its import for school relations. For this means that all learning is in an immanent mode, or the actualizations of so many possible resonances between teacher and taught. In other words, curriculum is not a given, nor even an interpretation or co-construction, as some modern theories would have it. Instead, what we have in this framework is a *becoming-curriculum*, like becoming-sorcerer that we saw earlier, that is an effort to release the intensities trapped in the signifiers. On this plane there is little distinction between teacher and learner. The student's becoming is in reciprocal presupposition with the teacher's becoming.

The setting of the school, its beginning, and its continued struggle to remain different within a bureaucratic space that attempts to reduce everything to identity bestows on it a certain sense of passion that is not simply the tension born of daily business. At weekly staff meetings, there are always questions, reservations, and contrary opinions about the directions the school is taking. More important, student views are actively sought, discussed, and taken into consideration in determining curricular directions. In a recent vote on a vacant slot for a course, seniors voted to learn Latin. Some of them thought learning Latin was "cool." Urban kids voting to learn Latin took even staff at the school, used to unpredictability, by surprise. As a result, there is a distinctly nebulous quality, a becoming that is uncertain and has a mitigating effect on the strict boundaries that define teacher and student roles in larger, more impersonal settings where difference gets reduced or forced into the violence of identity.

Deleuze claims that dogged identities are the product of an "arborescent model" of thought, a proud tree model of hierarchic representation that replicates the established order. I am a teacher because the statute book has laid down the model of a teacher and I am a replica of that model. In repetition there is certainty. The "arborescent" order functions on the basis of resemblance—on likeness to the model of the good student, or the model of the good teacher, a derivation of the Platonic "image-copy" or repetition. Its modus operandi is negation: If you are not a good student, then you are a poor student ($X = X = $ not Y). There are clear outlines and categories that one must fit, or fall into an alternative category. Such spaces thickened into strata by repetition demand clear and constant reinforcement of boundaries for the purpose of not losing control, for lines of delineation are also borders that control possibilities of movement.

The relatively fluid space at the school, however, does not mean that teachers here give up their adult roles and become indistinguishable from adolescents. As M.S., a senior teacher, observes: "Some people come in thinking, 'I want to be their friend'; I have been through that phase myself. But [students] don't want that, they want you to be the *adult*...the caring but firm grown-up. They want to feel the boundaries." (Interview with M.S. No.1) Thus, it is much more complex than simply a question of dissolving *all* boundaries. The boundaries are also becoming, that is, transforming in response to ongoing processes. It is not difference or repetition, but difference *and* repetition. It is what Deleuze calls the "molar" within the "molecular" or "striated" spaces within "nomad" territory, implying that there are and must be regulated spaces within more open territory and that one has to pay attention to both because the binary is always breaking down—controlled spaces lose their boundaries at critical moments and open territories become bounded and reified over time.

As I look and listen, it appears that the school is groping toward a different order for which it does not yet have a language. It has a certain appreciation of difference and leaky spaces in the context of which I feel teachers might profitably embrace a Deleuzian perspective that yields theoretical power and praxeological alternatives. Specifically, theorizing these openings or introducing the concepts we have been discussing might improve the quality of correspondence between the existing faculty and new teachers. How so? Because we meet in open territory or smooth space where multiplicities interact rather than strata attempting to dominate other strata. But I must be cautious here. I do not mean to suggest a divide between theory and practice; not only is that contrary to the notion of praxis, but Deleuze (1977) argues against any such distinction:

> Practice is a set of relays from one theoretical point to another, and theory is a relay from one practice to another....No theory can develop without eventually encountering a wall, and practice is necessary for piercing this wall. (206)

Therefore, when I talk about injecting Deleuzian concepts, I mean inserting into the pressures and flows of the school a fresh set of tools that are themselves nothing but intensities, and not the implementation of any theory.

To continue the discussion on boundaries, the sense of fluidity, or rather the partial loss of hard boundaries, at the school is also perhaps due to the fact that identity here is based more on *difference* than on *repetition*. By that I mean to say, students are not treated, either in the corridor or in the classroom, as a faceless mass, or a youthful gang that has to be contended with and made pliant, like in larger schools. Within the multiplicities, the pedagogy works to affirm difference: Mark, responsible for computer literacy at an adult literacy center, or Casey, working at the law office. These differences contribute to the reduced reliance on resemblance or representation as a guide to action.

In some cases I see the inchoate stirrings of the "nomadic." Systematic challenge to identitarian drives can generate what Deleuze calls nomadic space. Some of the staff go way beyond the call of duty to accommodate students' needs. In Massumi's words, "Nomad thought replaces the closed equation of representation (I = I = not you) with an open" expression that might look like: I + you + her +...(Deleuze and Guattari, 1987, xiii); that is to say, it creates open patchworks rather than closed boundaries. Recent staff meetings have brought up the whole question of leadership and whether the school was lapsing into the usual pattern of increasing reliance on one person to carry out leadership duties: "I am prepared to do full-time teaching, let someone else do this [administration]" said M.S., who has been handling most of the administrative tasks in the lead teacher's role. (Field Notes 04/19/02). Here we see brief evidence of a different kind of rhizomatic sensibility emerging, a tense but dynamic interplay of power relationships that are not solely linear. It is a somewhat open patchwork that we see here, on which a Deleuzian lens can operate to generate new possibilities. The immediate response to the situation is a stepping back by M.S. that creates room for new affiliations. It can also be seen as a challenge to the liberal-technocratic vision that rests on the ideology of possessive individualism. The ability to step back from ownership has its echoes elsewhere too. A minor deterritorializing movement in this direction is evidenced in the way in which teachers are sometimes willing to give up some of their personal time in the interests of the students. A rhizome cannot be confined within linear coordinates; it tends to produce its own temporal expansions and contractions within relations. M.S. observes:

> Sometimes I have to work during weekends and the evenings because the students are in all kinds of placements. We are not in a position to make those clear distinctions here between personal time and school time, but we try to be fair in load distribution. (Interview with M.S. No.2)

This attitude makes a minor dent in the ideal of possession, the clear boundaries of the mine and the yours. Popkewitz (1988) has remarked:

> The view of society as composed by "possessive" individuals provides a basis for organizing schooling. Attitudes, knowledge, and skills were conceived of as personal property of the individual. The psychology of a possessive individual is incorporated into contemporary curriculum through the use of behavioral objectives and psychological testing and measurement. Methods of teaching are to enable individuals to develop particular attributes and abilities and to internalize some logical state which

they "own" as one would objects or commodities. (86)

The conventional organization of schooling is predicated on the idea of the possessive individual that includes the domination of space and of specific roles within it. But the strength of the rhizome is that it has no center. The resultant patchwork is a quickening of intensities in an immanent field, and a new micropolitics emerges: a politics of becoming that invents a new plane. While not everyone, especially novice teachers, feels positive about the loss of boundaries, and some feel oppressed by this disappearing line, it is certainly a challenge to established ways of doing things. Besides, it is a step toward a qualitative multiplicity as a driving force of organization.

But connectedness to the multiplicities does not mean the actors become amorphous or lose any of their sense of personal identity. A useful metaphor for thinking about this kind of multiplicity is the "pack." Elias Canetti has written that in a pack each member is alone even as they participate closely in the activities of the group: "In the changing constellation of the pack, in its dances and expeditions, he will again and again find himself at its edge. He may be in the center and then, immediately afterwards at the edge again. As the pack forms a ring around the fire…each man's back is naked and exposed to the wilderness" (Deleuze and Guattari, 1987, 33–34). This sense of being in the group and yet having one's back exposed is peculiarly present here. Deborah Meier (1995) has observed that it comes partly from the dangers and the lived uncertainties of urban conditions. It is important for new teachers to appreciate this dual movement and not see them as opposed. Pedagogy is apt to undergo change when a teacher actually comes into contact with the arising of identity within multiplicities.

MS says, "Every little thing affects the whole school" (Interview with M.S. No.2). In other words, there are no isolated occurrences. This recognition that each encounter has consequences for the entire school shows how discrete categories break down replaced by a web of connectedness. In striated space or on a State grid, encounters are assumed to take place in isolation with local effects only. But in smooth space there are no isolated points, only neighborhoods that are in proximal relationships. Such an approach leads to a very different response to, say, the manner in which disciplinary issues are handled, among other things. There are no detentions or suspensions here, a fact that novice teachers often find problematic, nor is there an administrative hierarchy that takes care of disciplinary issues. The thing must be handled on the pedagogical plane within less rigid stratifications or hierarchies.

Grassroots Organization

The City School teachers believe that what young people need most, in the kind of school they have created, are "sane adults" in whose presence "students feet safe," who are "willing to listen to them," and with whom they can hold conversations without the feeling of "being judged all the time." I asked D.N., one of the teachers, what the term "sane" meant to him in this context. He said, for him it was "people who were willing to move away from fixed positions" while dealing with issues (Interview with D.N. No.1). Phil, a fifteen-year-old, was expelled from his previous school. His story of the events that led to his expulsion is as follows:

> Phil lives with his grandmother and earns for the two of them working evenings after school. Being ill last winter he was absent from school for a week; and then his grandmother fell ill. Being unwell himself, Phil had to take his grandmother down to Texas to some relatives. On return, he found that they had struck his name off most of the classes that were important to him, and wouldn't let him back in. When he protested, one teacher dismissed him saying he was "totally irresponsible." Enraged, he yelled back and was promptly thrown out. No one, Phil claims, was willing to hear his side of the story (Journal Entry No.14).

State space is also mutilated silence. Deleuze (1977) remarks, "If the protests of children were heard in kindergarten, if their questions were attended to, it would be enough to explode the entire educational system" (209). Deleuze is suggesting that so-called reforms attend to false problems, never paying attention to those who are actually affected by the school system. In State space one can move only along approved gridded points that rarely allow students the voice with which to speak. This could not have happened to him at his present school, Phil asserts: "Here, they listen to you...most of the time" (Field Notes 04/17/02). In this context, recall the debate about changing the name of the school. It seems to lend credence to Phil's assertion that students here have a chance to be heard.

The right to speak for oneself is not a move toward identity but always already a multiplicity. It is the "indignity of speaking for others" that affirms representationalism (Deleuze, 1977, 209). Deny representation, and add it to multiple voices, and you have the rhizome. The rhizome is contrasted with arborescent systems, that is, with roots and trees, that, according to Deleuze, "fix an order" and are thereby restrictive and authoritarian. The image of the tree with its linear hierarchy is present everywhere in Western thought (the tree of knowledge, the tree of lineage, etc.), which denies multiplicity; there is very little lateral movement. Rhizomes, instead, slide laterally; tubers or mosses spread sideways and grow from the edges at any point.

Selena and Jennifer, two seniors, are offering a semester-long course on Greek mythology. The class is full. They demonstrate a surprising depth of knowledge on the subject. Observing these two students take on the role of the teacher and co-teach is an object lesson. J.C., a teacher, says, "This is a *grassroots* organization. Our students are often prepared to take on these things" (Field Notes 05/06/02). For Deleuze, grass is rhizome, grows through the cracks, and "in between" the cracks. The grassroots metaphor is therefore strikingly apt. Here one identifies the possibility of a deeper deterritorialization that would provide more cracks of the sort through which Selena and Jennifer are operating.

Developing the metaphor of the rhizome further, in Deleuze these are collective assemblages of enunciation, heteroglossic chains of every kind that bring into play not only different regimes of signs but also states of things of different status. A rhizome "ceaselessly establishes connections between semiotic chains, organizations of power, and circumstances relative to [knowledges] and social struggles." Deleuze explains semiotic chains as tubers "agglomerating very diverse acts, not only linguistic, but also perceptive, mimetic, gestural, and cognitive" (Deleuze and Guattari, 1987, 7). In other words, a rhizome cuts across boundaries between the discursive and the nondiscursive and directly acts upon the micropolitics of the social field. It is a virtuality that actualizes in concrete situations.

Also, it is the concept of the rhizome to which one can profitably appeal in order to understand a system that tries to function without a center or a clearly identifiable central authority. The school has no central arboreal structure, and can be held together only by making "ceaseless connections" between people, ideas, and materials, and through entanglements of concept, percept, and affect. This means pedagogy must invariably take into account voice.

Mentoring is part of this rhizomatic dispersion and links back to multiple connections. Asked to identify one key factor that played a role in his renewed interest in academics, Jardine, a senior at the school who had once dropped out, said it was the way teachers here mentored him and "were interested in his life." It had little to do with academics directly. It was as if he had suddenly "regained something," a side of him that was missing had rejoined him. M.S. observes that "in large urban schools students survive and sometimes even do well, but they do it by shutting out a part of themselves" (Interview with M.S. No.2). In Deleuzian terms, the rhizomatic multiplicity of ourselves is forced into arboreality with the resultant loss of intensity. M.S. suggests that it is only by severing certain pathways and ways of connecting to the world around them that students are able to remain within the restricted domain where State space puts them. In a conversation with Foucault, Deleuze (1977) writes that in State space, "Not only are prisoners treated like children, but children are treated like prisoners. [They] are submitted to an infantilization which is alien to them" (210). There is less evidence at this school of this infantilization or humiliating treatment that Deleuze speaks of.

Engaging Signs
"I am always having to read students' auras," laughs M.S. (Interview with M.S. No.2). Several things in this utterance are remarkable. First, it is unusual to hear a reference to "auras" in mainstream discourse of schools. Auras are not objectively observable; they are esoteric, uncertain, and according to the literature, have fuzzy boundaries. Metaphorically, the "aura" that M.S. attempts to "read" is not only a reference to the occult personality that hides behind the visage but also an acknowledgment of the uncertainty of its boundaries, and a degree of mutability that is inherent in the educational encounter. For the aura has to be *"read,"* according to M.S., which I take to mean "interpreted," and does not disclose itself as transparent self-presence. The reference to the aura is thus also an indirect

acknowledgment of the presence of the absent. It is an important indication of the impossibility of reducing everything to the simplistic grid of techno-managerial space. The value of such a reading is that it leaves room for the student's becoming in the encounter, of the possibilities of realizing unsuspected relationalities that striated space excludes in its reinforcing of rigid boundaries.

But "[e]very rhizome contains lines of segmentarity according to which it is stratified, territorialized, organized...as well as lines of deterritorialization down which it constantly flees" (Deleuze and Guattari, 1987, 9). Elena, who is also a teenage mother, has not fared too well academically. Her placement is at NH Academy, a private school. CM and I talk to her placement mentor, who is full of praise for Elena:

She has developed a full schedule for herself here, teaching library skills and tutoring math. But what is remarkable is that she has this strange way of communicating with the girls. We have some middle-school girls who give trouble to some teachers. Elena just pulls them aside and talks to them and they listen to her. She has become an advocate for them with their teachers as well. (Field Notes 04/09/02)

From a critical angle, it is unclear whether Elena's efforts at enhancing communication between students and teachers by means of a certain advocacy and informal advising is empowering for the girls or is complicit in further extending the teachers' authority over them. But seen from a Deleuzian perspective, it is not necessary to "clarify" or comprehend Elena's position as either empowering or subordinating, but the question instead is whether the girls find new ways of expressing and communicating, that is, new ways of becoming in conjunction with her efforts.

For acts of freedom and acts of capture go on side by side. There is no dichotomy, only selections, says Deleuze. That is to say, although hidden in every rhizome is also "oedipal resurgences and fascist concretions," that is, the possibility of slipping into centrist movements, we can choose to focus on the deterritorializing aspect, being aware at all times of the reterritorializing movement. In terms of the above example, while Elena's acts may be liberatory and hegemonic at the same time, we choose to focus on the creative possibilities while alertly watching for the other movement. New boundaries come up all the time, even as the effort goes on to hold the existing ones open and flexible. A constructivist curriculum may contain in its bosom modernist assumptions even while attempting to escape from it.

Therefore, there is no question of forming a "dualist opposition," as Deleuze points out, between unitariness and multiplicity. Trees have rhizome lines, and rhizomes have points of arborescence. "How could," asks Deleuze, "mad particles be produced with anything but a gigantic cyclotron? How could lines of deterritorialization be assignable outside of circuits of territoriality?" (Deleuze and Guattari, 1987, 34). Both State space and nomad territory need the other for definition and for action. What state philosophy tries to do is to bring under control the unmanageable existence, but in the process of doing so, it reifies the reference points, thus reducing existence to a grid. Nomad thought, which is its Outside, must reintroduce multiplicity to free thought from the death grip of gridded existence.

At their placements, some of the students display a singularly different disposition. One student, a surly youth disconnected from academics and at times facing difficulties in school relationships, is a very different person when he enters the elementary classroom where he is placed. The children obviously adore him and he is absorbed in his work with them. Watching him stand there loosely, talking with staff at the placement facility, one notices the emergence of a different person. State space denies this multiplicity.

Also, what the vision of multiplicity urges is a cross-fertilization between zones that needs to be explored more thoroughly by the teachers than it is at the moment. While the languages of the placements intermingle at a certain level with the language of the school, a more substantial cross-use of the different sets of enunciations is often not there. For instance, the stories of students' experiences can enter into a "rhizome" with the rest of the curriculum; these narratives can reach into the micropolitics of public formation at the school. We even form a rhizome with our viruses, says Deleuze, that transport genetic material between species, thus making it impossible to draw definite lines between species. In this instance, the "genetic material" would be field material available daily once students are trained to be careful observers and biographers, a task that invokes the emphasis on autobiography in

Pinar's (1995) and Grumet's (1988) work. Through material drawn from the field and connected to the school curriculum, learning becomes cross-fertilized, exchanging material along many lines, as will be clear from the following example.

Rhizome and Resistance

A field visit to the local newspaper office turns out to be instructive in a surprising manner. We sit around, and the editor holds forth on a special issue he is bringing out on alternative schools: addressing issues on teenage pregnancy, drug abuse, etc. Macy whips around angrily: "Did you hear how he said "teenage mothers"? What's he know about teenage motherhood? I'm a teenage mom and am proud of it. Wouldn't give it up for nothing. I love my baby" (Field Notes 04/27/02). With these words, Macy impugns the patronizing discourse about teenage pregnancy, and a new plateau of intensity emerges showing the poverty of the discourse. I am witnessing a living curriculum. Macy spotting patriarchy, Macy grappling with monolithic patriarchy, Macy resisting with her multiplicity, with her right to be a student + a mother + a teenager +....

Observing A.D., I realized that he was focused entirely on what the editor had to say, and had not paid attention to what Macy said in response. The editor represented for A.D. the source of authentic utterance, thus keeping the situation tied to strong categorical relationships. Macy's outburst could help reconvene the murmurs and "stammerings" that Deleuze constantly alludes to in his writings (Deleuze and Parnet, 1987), and the curricular possibilities and connectivities that could emerge out of that experience. A.D. seemed more focused on the formal aspects of "what the students learned," that is, on *recovering* what was given in the newspaper office, rather than actively seeking the embodied perceptions of students. In the process, he misses what the differential perceptions produced and the rhizomatic connections that surrounded him. Part of the challenge of an innovative curriculum is to continually turn situations into learning opportunities; we must produce the curriculum in conjunction with becoming, or rather, there is a becoming-curriculum as might have occurred if A.D. had allowed himself to be deterritorialized by Macy's stand. This is not the same thing as what is often called a "student-centered approach," and it certainly isn't a teacher-centered one. Instead, this is an *acentered*, rhizoid approach.

That is to say, it has no center; it urges us to conceive of learning and perception in terms of constructing rhizoid spaces. This partly means we recuperate within thought, as much as possible of the intensities and resonances that become available by going beyond the signifier. And this, in turn, means remaining ever vigilant about the production of signs. This vigilance is not the self-conscious awareness of any autonomous being—for that would plunge us right back into the trap of humanism—but a subpersonal and strategic deployment of passion.

But this passion, from where does it come? It arises from the hand-to-hand combat with the forces of signification that I elaborate on in the following chapter, forces that turn into structures of power and stratification once they occupy certain sign regimes. Even as these forces occupy the signs, they produce the "forgetting" of their conditions of emergence and become normalized. To prevent this normalization is passion. This is the battle we have to fight, of throwing off, not accumulating, of shedding and not acquisition. It is through loss, Deleuze has reminded us, rather than acquisition that we gather the necessary momentum for transformation.

Conclusion

As I investigated the curricular and learning relationships in the school, it seemed to me that the problem novice teachers faced in finding their feet in this fluid environment could be seen as a semiotic problem: that of getting away from signifying regimes that project the signs of learning as bounded, convergent, and a function of representation, toward experimenting with differential possibilities within repetition, and multiple ways of making connections that continually undergo change and reveal unexpected and irregular learning opportunities. I have suggested throughout that a Deleuzian praxis can help teachers constructively come to terms with their own category constructs as well as the somewhat open and indeterminate spaces in the school that provide new openings for the play of signs. In the next chapter, I discuss ways of taking this deterritorialization, or undermining the existing order, further through a semiotic exercise of experimenting with signs in a Deleuzian manner, an exercise I call "apprenticeship of the sign." Umberto Eco (1980) remarks that signs are all we have to orient us in this world. Signs may keep us pinned down to existing ways and relations, or they can be engaged in a very different manner that displaces us from the world of representation onto a differential plane. Therefore, a lot depends on how we engage and experiment with signs. I claim that investigating the sign reconfigures some of the constricting boundaries that have become reified and normalized in the teachers' lifeworld.

What follows are some ways in which teachers can reexamine the signs that arise in the educational encounter and experience themselves not as something outside the production of the sign, that is as something transcendent, but as an *entanglement*, or as part of the generation of the sign itself, that is, as immanence. In this way we move from the transcendent plane to one of immanence in which we are always implicated in the signs that we observe. In other words, we realize our productive role in the generation of the sign, which leads to a more active and responsible mode of being. For it is akin to saying that we are partly responsible for the reality that we perceive. The Deleuzian pragmatics is thus a profoundly ethical struggle.

Notes

1. The molar and the molecular have nothing to do with size. The atom is a molar entity, while a sand dune might be a molecular entity—individual sand particles may be blown off and deposited elsewhere during a sandstorm. Therefore, these are not distinctions of scale but consist of qualitative differences in the manner in which they are composed. Molecular compositions manifest strictly local connections, and thus are capable of continuous variation, whereas molar compositions are rather more restricted, being trapped as a result of geologic action or cultural images of unification. But this is not a strict dichotomy. It is possible to be poised in the threshold between the molar and the molecular, that is, to have boundaries that are flexible and open to change.

2. Take a phenomenon such as the birth of a planet. A cloud of dust begins to coalesce in the presence of certain synthesizing forces, or "attractors," such as, for example, the gravitational field of a young

star. By means of stochastic processes of selection, the different layers are formed, with some of the dust included and some left out. At each stage, different discriminating forces capture suitable material and act upon the different strata to form yet other strata. The result of all this immense activity is present in the end as an apparently unified entity. The fluctuating field of volatile gas and dust has solidified into a stable unity, and the individual particles, themselves composites, are temporarily locked in, and can now behave only as strata.

Starting from the opposite end, consider an "event" such as the French Revolution. Once we get past the label that identifies "it" historically, it becomes impossible to localize it or see it as something unified with a clear boundary. There are too many things going on for there to be a center that can be clearly identified. Further, Latour (1993) notes that French historians have recently discovered that "the actors and chroniclers of 1789 used the notion of revolution...to influence their own fate" (40). In other words, the revolution was being produced in part by the idea of revolution. It is the lack of a unifying center that makes all phenomena multiplicities.

3. The a-signifying semiotic is a transformation or a particle of intensity that has not yet been captured by any signifying regime. In other words, it is an in-between state where meaning is fluid and has not settled down or stratified.

Chapter 4

The Apprenticeship

The nomads are the ones who don't move on, they become nomads because they refuse to disappear.　　　　　　— A. Toynbee cited in *A Thousand Plateaus*

In the previous chapter we saw the manner in which the learning activities and needs of the actors in the school as well as their identities leaked out of the regular and more circumscribed spaces onto irregular territory, as also the difficulty novice teachers faced in contending with complexity and difference that arose in those spaces. In the language of our analysis, the novice teachers continued in the stream of "overcoding" or assimilation that subsumes difference and attempts to produce universals of meaning according to established values and modes of thinking. Observing that difference and divergence, and not representational certainty, must be central to a more pertinent response to what was going on at the school, I offered the Deleuzian notion of the rhizome not only as a descriptive tool but also as a praxis, as a way of conceiving interactions in terms of becoming. For as I have said earlier, who we are, that is, the image we have of ourselves, is inextricably linked with how we formulate our interactions. I argued that rhizomatic thinking would be able to respond more adequately to the volatile and indefinitude of urban education in particular. But for this shift to occur, actual experimentation is necessary.

In this chapter, we will take the work of reconceptualizing the pedagogical encounter a step further, and investigate in general the sign systems in which we are implicated. As teachers, we must do the work of creating hollows from where we can speak without being overcoded, that is, assimilated into existing sign regimes. I suggest that a fundamental rethinking or reconceptualizing of the ways in which we construct learning, and the image of ourselves that is dispersed in it, cannot happen without a certain experimentation and praxeological exercise that opens up these orders. In other words, it needs a hand-to-hand combat with signs, for all percepts and constructs are made up of signs that arise between perceiver and perceived, between observer and environment (Deleuze, 1972; Luhmann, 1990; Bateson, 1991). Deleuze (1972) observes:

> Learning is essentially concerned with *signs*. Signs are the object of a temporal apprenticeship, not of an abstract knowledge. To learn is first of all to consider a substance, an object, a being as if they emitted signs....Everything which teaches us something emits signs, every act of learning is an interpretation of signs or hieroglyphs. (4)

This seems at first to evoke a classic hermeneutic position. However, as we shall see, Deleuze takes us in a very different direction and into the sign itself, to enter it, to take apart the singularities of its composition, and along with Guattari (1984), moves into a pre-signifying field of flux.

This chapter, then, sets itself the task of inquiring into the complexity of the sign from a Deleuzian perspective, and offers a certain semiotic experimentation which a practitioner might undertake so as to be able to insinuate oneself into differential spaces. In order to construct such a conceptual apparatus, I offer here a mode of experimentation that I call an *apprenticeship of the sign* that allows us to uncover the nuances of signs. It is argued here that for teachers entering into the profession, it is important to become apprenticed to the sign; to become what Deleuze (1972) calls "Egyptologists" of the signs generated in encounters so as to be able to continually escape the modes of dominant significations that reify knowledge. Therefore, a substantial part of the chapter is devoted to developing an experimental framework for studying signs, an endeavor which I have said in the introduction is a major purpose of the book; in the latter half of the chapter I use data from the case study to throw light on the working of the framework.

The framework developed here is also directed at the work of creating a matrix so as to be able to raise complex issues around teacher becoming and teacher education. Britzman and Dippo (1998) have pointed out, the question of teacher becoming must consider "complex conversations about...conflictive forms of knowledge, culture, identity, community, language..." without which inequalities in education will persist (15). For denial of complexity is the counterpart of denial of heterogeneity, and results in capitulating to social totalities and molar stratifications. In highly differentiated environments such as urban schools, to deny complexity is to abet hegemony.

But the apprenticeship takes the "complex conversation" in a somewhat different direction; it takes it underground, so to speak, to a subpersonal level, to the level of singularities and intensities, and to what Guattari (1984) has called an a-signifying semiotics:

> [The] position of the subject changes radically when a-signifying semiotics come to the forefront. The world of mental representation then no longer functions to over-encode semiotics. Signs are involved in things prior to representation. Signs and things engage each other independently of the subjective control...of individual utterances. (76)

The a-signifying semiotics takes us into a terrain beyond meaning, to sets of relations between force fields, to junctures where forces turn into power, clothing themselves in specific utterances that invent an interiority and a signified. This is vital from the point of education if we are to reinfuse life into curriculum. To get out from beneath signifier models that project a stable signified, and to get into a hand-to-hand combat with forces themselves, we have to get to

> a generalized micropolitical struggle that can undermine it from within, in such a way as to enable all the intensive multiplicities to escape from the tyranny of the signifying overcoding. What this means is unleashing a whole host of expressions and experimentations that all work to penetrate and eat into the semiology of the dominant order, to feel out new escape routes and produce new and unheard of constellations of a-signifying particle beams. (84)

This means that teachers have to learn to problematize what they are "seeing" and not fall into the trap of a naïve realism; they have to experience themselves as joint *producers* of the sign regimes in which they participate. This displacement in the mode of perception is attempted through the apprenticeship. The very ontological assumptions and boundaries that construct school and learning undergo a fresh examination once we become apprenticed to the sign. A new sense of looking and listening is urged on us by the realization that we are, at all times, implicated in the signs that we perceive. This brings about a fresh orientation in the educational encounter where the opposite end of the encounter, or the "Other" is no longer an absolute Other but an inescapable part of the signs that are jointly generated in the encounter.

Referring to Derrida's phrase *"Tout Autre est Tout Autre,"* Doll (1999) says: "The phrase is easily translatable as a truism 'every other is every other.' But it can mean...Every one is every bit other. The challenge then, ethically and educationally, is to work with this new notion of 'otherness,' to realize that as humans we are all other— generally and locally" (89). That is, we are at the same time self and alterity—difference and repetition. To put it differently, no identity is self-coincident, and most important, identity is produced always and only in an encounter. It is the clash of forces between the observer and the observed, each of which is implicated in the production of the other, that gives rise to the sensible, the sign. And it is the sign that we must learn to examine in this new way, that is, with the awareness of co-production, if we are to respond to the challenge of becoming aware that we are both self and other, difference *and* repetition. No longer is it possible to believe that the signs—the students that we face, the curriculum that is handed down to us, the concepts and language that we use—are independent of us. In this manner we "enter" the sign, as it were, and become implicated in it.

This complexifies the way we observe and react to things, and brings about a moment of diffidence, of creative hesitancy, between observation and recognition, producing a murmur or a "creative stammering," to use a Deleuzian concept (Deleuze and Guattari, 1987, 98). For no longer is the sign entirely outside of us. To go back to M.S.'s reference to auras:

K.R.: On quite a few occasions I have heard you refer to having to read students' auras. Can you clarify it a little for me what you mean by this process?

M.S.: Well, I don't mean anything very esoteric. It is a sort of intuitive grasp of symptoms they show.

K.R.: Are these symptoms entirely generated by the student or are these subjective as well?

M.S.: I am not sure I understand. Do you mean whether I am imagining it?

K.R.: No. I mean do you see yourself only as a passive receptor of these symptoms?

M.S.: No, I think a lot of me comes into play, my experience and on, so in that sense it is subjective. (Interview with M.S. No.2)

The grouping of symptoms or signs is a creative act, something that happens *between* the student and the teacher. An explicit realization of this creative process changes our habits of thought and the construction of relations, and we *become every bit Other*.

The creative moment of hesitancy or stammering brought about by the realization that we are implicated in the signs we experience is a minor but important surge of destratification; it opens up a space for moving away from repetition and toward a careful experimentation with signs. It helps us set aside our habitual, everyday mode of apprehending reality, and we begin to read signs as if in a "foreign language" (Deleuze, 1995, 133), which is the breaching of the old boundaries and divisions, producing minor disorientations and dissident flows in an otherwise repetitious reality. I suggest that a reorientation in thought's relation to signs in terms of a "foreign language," that is, not in terms of recognition, is facilitated by an experiment such as the apprenticeship of the sign. In the following pages, I aim to show what this involves and develop a framework for such an apprenticeship. Having set the context in the previous chapters, we begin here the work of praxis in a more formal manner.

Praxis

It will be necessary, before going any further, to dwell for a moment on what we mean by the *sign*. One way to talk about signs is to say they are aggregates of differences by which a perceiving organism is able to orient itself. Bateson (1991) observes that the key question at any given moment of the life of an organism is: What's happening? In an effort to respond to this existential question, the organism makes certain moves, and encounters differences that constitute information. Broadly speaking, then, a sign is anything that brings about a perception of change, difference, or information. From Bateson's perspective, it is a difference that makes a difference to any perceiving system.

But in Deleuze (1983), we find a radicalization of the sign. Signs are not merely the passive purveyors of difference, but the result of an active clash of forces; a sign is an event in and of itself:

> A phenomenon is a sign, a symptom which finds its meaning in an existing force. The whole of philosophy is a symptomatology, and a semiology. (3)

Further, "a sign is what flashes across the boundary of two levels, between two communicating series" (Deleuze, 1990b, 261). The sign, in this view, is, therefore, simply an arena for the struggle of forces, emerging when one set of forces overwhelms another, and it is in this sense I will use it here. The same object, phenomenon, or sign changes sense depending on the force which appropriates it, and therefore my focus will be on the becoming of the sign, on the forces that appropriate it, rather than on signification; that is, on emergence and construction rather than recognition. To read signs is to reconvene the unsaid, to stutter in a foreign language, to construct a language of difference.

As we have seen, the plane of representation cuts off the becoming of multiplicities, which is a mutant space or a plane of difference. That is to say, it hinders our understanding of the multiplicity of forces that occupy a sign at any moment because the drive is toward recognition through resemblance. Our attempt is to reconstruct the sign, to enter the sign itself and *become* with the sign in an immanent fashion, situated in the plane of the sign. To recount our major purpose, it is the formulation of certain conceptual tools for ways of looking, thinking, and experimenting that loosens the grip of existing boundaries and categories. Ceaseless problematization of signs is one way to prevent boundaries from closing in on us.

"Experiment," says Deleuze to the apprentice, "don't signify and interpret! Find your own places, territorialities, deterritorializations, regime, lines of flight! Semiotize yourself instead of rooting around in your prefab childhood" (Deleuze and Guattari, 1987, 139). To semiotize ourselves is to ride the differential of the sign into a conjuring space, and redistribute our intensities in conjunction with other intensities that are in resonance, a fashioning of the self after Foucault (1994), a practice of freedom that alters our sensibilities. To attempt a praxeological analysis therefore, or to serve an "apprenticeship of the sign," I will offer next a four-part analytical frame and illustrate its working through examples from the case study. I propose this as an aid to thinking and experimenting on sign regimes that bring about a change in our relationship to signs, and help us to be situated at the level of the signs themselves without seeking a transcendental viewpoint. The following are the four aspects of the praxis proposed here: 1. The Adscension; 2. The Alloscension; 3. The Amnioscension; and 4. The Anascension. I will explain each of these components below.

1. Adscension. Recall the Deleuzian critique of Platonism that was discussed in chapter 2. I observed that Platonism, or the drive toward universals and the subsumption of difference under identitarian schemas or assimilationism, is an underpinning of most modernist institutions, and of schooling in particular. Curriculum caught in Platonic ideals ignores or fails to notice differential experience. This element of the praxis helps to carry forward the work of reversing Platonism that we began earlier. It alerts us to what Deleuze calls "the points of subjectivation" (Deleuze and Parnet, 1987, 114) where signs begin to coagulate toward specific and dominant significations.

And here we must introduce Plato's notion of the simulacra which is seized by Deleuze in order to turn Platonism on its head. In the Platonic schema of the world as *icon* or model, and objects as copies, the notion of the simulacrum is evoked in order to distinguish between good and bad copies. For Plato, simulacra are false copies or phantasms and a threat to the purity of the genuine types. But according to Deleuze (1990b), the simulacrum is neither model nor copy:

> The simulacrum is not a degraded copy. It harbors a positive power which denies *the original and the copy, the model and the reproduction*. At least two divergent series are internalized in the simulacrum—neither can be assigned as the original, neither as the copy. (262)

In other words, Deleuze denies the model-copy reading of the world, and instead, posits the world itself as phantasm, as succession of images based on disparity, dissymmetry, and difference. In fact one recalls Bateson's (1991) famous assertion that it is difference that makes a difference, affirming the point that dissymmetry or the differential is the basic condition of the production of a distinction or information. The subtle mechanism of this production process is as follows. Deleuze explains that heterogeneous or divergent series—of unformed matter/singularities/frequencies—when juxtaposed set up "internal resonance" which "go beyond the series themselves" (261). This resonance generates a positive force or movement that gives rise to the simulacrum:

> This simulacrum includes the differential point of view; and the observer becomes part of the simulacrum itself, which is transformed and deformed by his point of view. In short, there is in the simulacrum...a becoming unlimited [that is] always more or less at once but never equal. (258) [1]

So, the emergence of the simulacra or objects of the world is not from an ideal type which hovers over the process but from the attraction between myriad and multiplicity of forces that act on one another in a contingent fashion. It becomes clear now why we had to introduce the notion of the simulacra. The communicating series can communicate only because of potential difference, and therefore the observer, who is nothing but another series and not necessarily human, becomes part of the production of the simulacrum, that is, part of the simulacrum itself. It is in the becoming of the simulacra that there is a freedom which triumphs over icons and models. It is here that we find an affirmation of difference.

No doubt, we still have the experience of resemblance, but "the same and the similar no longer have an essence except as simulated" (262). That is to say, the effect of resemblance comes not from the interiority of model or icon but is "completely external," produced by the manner in which a sign flashes across the "dissymmetries" of the two communicating series. In other words, the experience of sameness and resemblance is not due to any internal invariance but to the whole pattern of differences that are repeated.

Hence, to experiment with different series and internalize their constitutive dissymmetries is a first step in our work. The next step is to see ourselves as not identities but as generating discrepancy and dissimilitude that resonate with other discrepant or divergent series; we, therefore, *perceive ourselves as simulacrua*. In tracking the movement of signs or the clash of forces in the everyday, and in pedagogic encounters, we become aware of the indefinite nature of the series of thought-feeling-utterance that we call identity, and the sea of the unformed and the unsaid from which arises a particularity as an "evaporative surface effect" (Massumi, 1992, 46). This radically alters our attitude toward the pedagogic encounter, and we can no longer remain embedded in the struggle for producing resemblance. Instead of seeking the safe but illusory ground of identity and similitude, we seek to produce difference.

It is important to clarify that sign regimes are not to be confused with language. Instead, they are "fluxes of expression and fluxes of content" and "language is never the only flux of expression" (Deleuze and Parnet, 1987, 117). Therefore, language is only one aspect of assemblages of enunciation. For Deleuze, signs have as much to do with the extratextual as with text. It is through careful attention to the sign and a persistent awareness of the generative factor that we begin to lose the sense of reality as concrete and given, and therefore change becomes possible.

To recap then, adscension is a praxeological move in which we identify the points of subjectivation of signs, that is, step back from dominant or ideal significations to observe the rise of the simulacra. In the process of observing the world as simulacra, our identities loosen up and we become more sieve-like rather than closed entities. This is an important step that takes us away from molar categories.

2. Alloscension. The next element or function shows how one regime of signs gets translated into another, that is, with what "transformations, residues, variations, and innovations" change comes about. It would show "not simply how semiotics mix, but how new semiotics are detached and produced, and how they inspire new assemblages" and mutants (Deleuze and Parnet, 1987, 114). Experimentation with transformation or mutation shows us how reality is produced out of mutating sign regimes. To take an example,

We may ask when statements of the Bolshevik type first

appeared and how Leninism, at the time of the break with the
social democrats, effected a veritable transformation that created
an original semiotic....In an exemplary study, Jean-Pierre Faye
did a detailed analysis of the transformations that produced
Nazism, viewed as a system of new statements in a social field.
(Deleuze and Guattari, 1987, 139)

Taking a different example, we can find out how the dominant
discourses in the school have been produced, that is, the conditions of
their emergence. It is crucial for the apprentice to become aware of
these births and transformations, for they constantly lead us to view
how new regimes emerge from old ones, and what residues they
leave behind. These residues, no less than the emergent regimes,
define the boundaries of what we consider as reality.

In studying alloscension or transformation of sign regimes, it is
useful to make distinctions between several kinds. Transformations
that take sign regimes into a presignifying zone, that is, where the
privileged status of language is no longer ensured, are called
"analogic" by Deleuze. An example from the case study is M.S.'s
evocation and tracing of auras which have an "extratextual" aspect.
Following this line, we are led into a more unlimited zone where
things become fuzzy. Second, transformations that take signs into a
signifying zone, that is, where the signifier dominates and there is
uniformity of enunciation and expression, may be called "symbolic."
An example of this is L.S.'s insistence on the formal way of doing
science seen in the previous chapter. Here, the signs are overpowered
by dominant significations such as what is science learning. Third,
transformations that take sign regimes into a counter-signifying zone,
that is, into an oppositional frame, may be called "strategic." A
possible example of that zone might be Macy's rejection of the
editor's point of view that we saw in the previous chapter. Her series
of utterances clash with the editor's views that produce new
offshoots. Finally, there are transformations that take semiotics into a
postsignifying zone, that is, into mimicking consciousness itself, such
as we find in chapter 5, where a subject says she no longer knows
what her feelings are (Deleuze and Guattari, 1987, 135–36). In the
mimetic, we glimpse the limits of signification, and signs begin to
mime the unformed, the "chaos" from which a statement or utterance
appears as a surface effect. Close attention to these four aspects—the

analogic, the symbolic, the strategic, and the mimetic — sensitize us to
the processes of world-making through signification. We reconstellate
sense data by using our bodies as the experimental ground, and thus
bring about a more generative relationship with the "Outside."

In inserting ourselves thus into the semiotic process of alloscension,
we enter into a mode of transformation, as the former closed regimes
of signs show themselves to be mutants of previous regimes and so
on, thus throwing us off center and onto a plane of becoming.
According to Deleuze and Guattari (1987), becomings "have neither
culmination nor subject, but draw one another into zones of
proximity or undecidability; smooth spaces, composed from within
striated space" (507). From strong categories that bind us to strata,
and restrict our freedom to think and operate, we enter into
continuums of intensities that expand the horizon of possibilities in a
pluralistic direction.

3. Amnioscension. In the combat of forces, the arising or emergence
of the sign corresponds to a momentary cessation of becoming, a
fleeting stabilization of flux. In other words, the sign, in a sense, is an
arrestment of the flow of singularities. Inscribed or actualized in
bodies, these give rise to molar categories and striated or State space.
And as we have seen, escape from these limitations, which reconnects
to the flux, is the process of becoming molecular.[2] The separation
between perceiver and perceived or experiencer and experience
becomes fuzzy in molecularity, and the dualism between cogito and
consciousness is eroded.

Becoming, in Massumi's (1992) words, is a "tension between modes
of desire" that outlines a new range of "potential relations" in the in-
between spaces "between two molar coordinates" (94). In other
words, as desire struggles between linearity and molecularity, there
appears for an instant the line of acceleration, a second order change,
which momentarily deterritorializes through a critical stimulus at a
sensitive moment. This happens in the smallest of intervals, in a kind
of passage to the limit. The most subversive kind of transformation is,
therefore, contrary to popular notions, not necessarily the largest and
the most grandiose, but the almost invisible fracture, the
instantaneous that can annihilate old structures. This is why, in the
third part of the praxis, we pay attention to the small interval:

The smallest interval is always diabolical. It is as though an

intense matter or a continuum of variation were freed...The idea
of the smallest interval does not apply to figures of the same
nature; it implies at least a curve and a straight line, a circle and a
tangent. (Deleuze and Guattari, 1987, 108)

The smallest deviation is produced when the curve turns away ever
so slightly from the tangent to the curve at a point, that is, when two
dissimilar figures or planes meet. The use of mathematical metaphor
is justified here since, in the smallest interval, the distinctions between
the biological, the mathematical, and the linguistic or informational
disappear.[3] What remains are intensities that occur in the smallest of
intervals, and that find no expression in ordinary language; that is to
say, they shatter language and form, freeing pure intensities. That is
why small changes that produce *secret lines of disorientation* are highly
effective.

In this manner, beneath the vast movements of regulated discourse
that correspond to the social attitudes and positions maintained by
the order-word, we come upon uncertain terrain, an indeterminate in-
between-ness of sensations, feelings, thoughts, gestures, and things
that cannot be forced into any category; we find excruciatingly small
gaps in which we may insert an impossible question, an aporia
through which to escape to new becomings. It is not a question of
evading the order-word, as Deleuze has pointed out, but to develop
its own power of escape.

The amnioscension is this meditation on the small interval that
holds the possibility of a revolutionary release of intensities. It
requires a careful reorientation in thought, a hanging on to minute
distinctions in space-time with one's fingernails as it were, without
being distracted by the large categories into which societal forces
thrust experience.

4. Anascension. Last, the apprentice must also know how to
recognize what Deleuze calls the "worldly sign." The "worldly sign"
is the empty sign, stereotypical and vacuous. It is the product of
inattention. It invents the stereotype and attempts to replace or "stand
in" for action and thought. It repeats, and "anticipates action as it
does thought, annuls thought as it does action" (Deleuze, 1972, 7).
Although empty, these signs are everywhere, and Deleuze says that
the apprenticeship would be incomplete if it did not pass through
them.

Pedagogically, signs that typecast the student coming from a difficult background as incapable, that see political resistance or dissent as intransigence, and signal differing abilities as failure, replace thought and action with empty vacuity. Nevertheless, to wake up fully to the sign, the apprentice must live through these vacant signs as well, and be aware that she or he is capable of producing the worldly sign which incapacitates.

The thing to grasp though is that the worldly sign itself is not the stereotype; it *invents* the stereotype. It has other potentialities or ways of becoming that are a pointer that any sign can begin to function like a worldly sign. This is connected to the key insight in *Difference and Repetition* (Deleuze, 1994), that repetition is not possible without difference. That is, what repeats is difference, and not the Same. So, even the worldly sign has the potentiality for escape, and we have to draw it out. It is only a lack of experimentation with the worldly sign that makes us fall into the trap of believing that it produces the same. One must enter its plane of becoming in order to see how it acts. But the real implication of the above is that, without constant watchfulness and experimentation, even deterritorialized signs can quickly become reterritorialized again. In other words, freed intensities can become locked once again into strata unless we remain engaged in the work of praxis.

With the help of the work outlined above, there comes about an intuition of the nomadic topos. The nomadic topos is never outside of us, but is part of our own self-description, a dynamic conjuring of new connectivities allowing new alignments freed from the stratification by order-words. The relentless examination of signs and our relationship to them opens up minor fissures, cracks, fault lines, and gaps through which fresh orientations and new imaginings become possible. These new imaginings are not necessarily new images but primarily a fluidation of reified images in thought. The apprenticeship therefore leads to what Deleuze and Guattari have called "schizoanalysis," referring to the possibility of minor schisis or fissure in our normal flows (Deleuze and Guattari, 1987, 146). "Minor" here does not mean unimportant, but rather, not readily discernible. Small changes or dissident flows may begin as a result of schizoanalysis, and minor flows of disorientation have the possibility of changing the habitus (Bourdieu, 1990), thus moving from relying on representation and recognition to difference and experimentation.

The four components of the praxis can generate a new image of ourselves as assemblages or compositions that can be recomposed at any time.

Britzman and Dippo (1998) have observed that the conventional approach to curriculum is to get teachers to move toward a more certain ground, toward more rigid planes, or in terms of our analysis, toward rigid "stratifications," through higher requirements, testing, certification, and so on. The teacher education and professionalization literature and the standards movement extol this objective side of teacher education. Being concerned with regulated spaces, they mostly do not take into account irregular becomings, the actual starts and stops, the faltering, the errors and accidents, desires, and other complexities that constitute complex learning. In contrast to the denial of complex thinking in conventional teacher education and curriculum in general (Britzman, 1998; Pinar, 2002), a Deleuzian analysis offers connections to the fields of indefinitude and flux from which events and identities appear as surface effects, mixing in new compositions, incorporeal transformations, and new opportunities for becoming. The ignoring of becoming, ignoring of moments of deterritorialization and flux, leads to great contradiction and to impotence, since what is ignored is precisely what we need to get people involved in their own becoming in education—a sense of becoming that is not merely a signifier on a grade sheet, but something palpable.

Case Analysis
Next, we will look at an example from the case study to see how the Deleuzian analysis can help to actualize the potential relations in the encounter. That is, by means of the exercise in semiotization outlined above, our effort will be to generate in the encounter a fleeting touch of the nomadic. The following is an excerpt from the Field Notes:

> This is a Friday seminar on journalism; the students are working on the school paper. All around me are signs of different kinds: linguistic, photographic, artistic, all being processed toward a final articulation. Some of the students are working on PCs edit-ing their pieces. According to the teacher, Carla has been uncoop-erative for some time, and her work has suffered. She is sitting in one corner frowning at some sketches. The top sketch shows two

apples baking in an oven talking to each other.

Teacher: Carla, these cartoons of yours, you'll have to explain to me what they mean.

Carla: [shrugs] I don't know. Cartoons don't have to mean any-thing.

Teacher: Probably 'mean' is not the right word. What do they indicate? What are you trying to say here?

Carla: [Pointing to a Calvin and Hobbes strip] What's this one mean here…a child and a stuffed toy?

Teacher: Now just a moment. You said "a stuffed toy." Is that just a stuffed toy to Calvin?

Carla: I don't know. Well, yes and no. I mean, He knows it's a stuffed toy…

Teacher: Yes?

Carla: He's also talking to him, and pretending it is talking back at him, so in some ways it's real to him I guess.

Teacher: So there are already two views right?

Carla: How does it make a difference? It's all in the author's head anyway.

Teacher: But animals communicate too. Children talk to animals all the time.

Carla: Only children and people who are screwed up.

Teacher: But you see the possibility of at least two perspectives? Why's that important here?

Carla: Yes…okay, it's like…there are different ways of looking at something.

Teacher: Alright, now let's look at your pieces. What is your perspective here?

Carla: [silent]

The discussion continued in an uneasy fashion with Carla partici-pating monosyllabically and becoming increasingly fidgety. (Field Note No.15)

There appear to be several things going on here—art, signs, representation, perspective, communication, resistance—several regimes of signs intercrossing, producing resonance and dissonance. As we discussed the situation afterwards, the teacher appeared to identify Carla's attitude as a typical case of disengagement, as someone going through the motions of school reluctantly, and indicated that there were other issues that compounded her behavior. The student-teacher encounter in itself was not problematized; instead, the teacher had taken a stance that corresponded to a molar categorization.

To reiterate, our purpose is to attempt a semiotization of the pedagogic encounter so that the heterogeneous series that emerge from encounters, as well as the resonance between their elements that are the result of difference and divergence could be seen as productive. In other words, what Saussure (1959) dismissed as the "heteroclite," or the seething elements untamed by language, are brought into our midst, thus deterritorializing dominant significations. Contemporary theorists such as Deborah Britzman and Henry Giroux have, from very different theoretical positions, already challenged the simplistic views by which the student is positioned as disengaged or disruptive. It will be helpful, as a contrastive device, to briefly allude to some of these positions in order to situate a Deleuzian analysis.

In her recent work in curriculum studies, Britzman (1998) has cast her arguments in terms of a Freudian ontology and epistemology, and works with the psychoanalytic assumption that education is necessarily an interference with the various unconscious desires of a child which give rise to fundamental conflicts not only between the learner and the teacher, but within the learner herself. Britzman (1998) observes:

> At the heart of psychoanalytic work is an ethical call to consider the complexity, conflicts, and plays of psyche and history. These are the conflicts—Eros and Thanatos, love and aggression—that education seems to place elsewhere. And these forces seem to come back to education as interruptions, as unruly students, as irrelevant questions, and as controversial knowledge in need of containment....The problem is that...How might educators begin to complicate not just the difficult knowledge on the outside but also the response to the difficult knowledge within—that other war? (133)

That "other war" Britzman refers to is the Freudian theater of the unconscious and its battle with the ego. The oversimplified modernist curriculum remains in denial of these complex dramas, and results in placing the difficult questions of life elsewhere, outside the realm of education. But these forces, so carefully kept out, come back to haunt the teacher in the classroom. They return in the form of interruptions, disengagement, and classroom battles, which give rise to feelings of oppression and irrelevance in the student and to a sense of hopelessness and defeat in the teacher.

Thus far, I go along with Britzman's position, but by tying her analysis to the twin forces of Eros and Thanatos of Freudian theory, Britzman directs attention to the psychological aspect of the *individual* rather than toward the subpersonal possibilities that arise in the in-between space of the learning encounter. Deleuze (1995) iterates his position with respect to Freud:

> What we're saying is that Freud at once discovers desire as libido, as productive desire, [but] is constantly forcing the libido back into a domestic representation within the Oedipus complex. (16)

The Oedipal theater rests within the individual unconscious, and therefore Carla's "oppositionality" in this framework must be seen as arising from the repressive mechanism of the Freudian position. But from a Deleuzian viewpoint, Carla's indifference or hostility can be seen as a problem of the in-between; it takes place in an encounter, and it is precisely this encounter which is the theater of production that must be theorized and not the individual unconscious. In other words, the teacher is implicated in it as much as the student.

I would like to examine the above data from yet another perspective before I proceed to the Deleuzian analysis with regard to this case. This time, we will look at it from the critical perspective of Henry Giroux, a curriculum theorist who may be seen as occupying a sort of borderland between critical theory and "postmodernism." Giroux is a significant commentator on contemporary urban youth, especially those whom he refers to as "border youth," and so is most pertinent in this case. Giroux (2000) has pointed out the "fractured condition" of the new generation of youth, as well as those who attempt to educate them, who are caught "between the borders of a modernist world of certainty and order, and a postmodern world of hybridized entities, electronic technologies, and local cultural practices" (176). In this shifting context, Giroux advocates a critical appropriation of postmodern pedagogic practices and a strategic engagement with modernism for a transformative political project in education.

Criticizing the "racially coded cultural legacy" of modernist schooling, which valorizes the experiences of the middle class, Giroux notes:

> The modernist nature of public schooling is evident in the refusal of educators to incorporate popular culture into the curricula or to take into account the…massively new socializing contexts for contemporary youth. (178)

The fact that education has not been able to come to terms with popular culture, and has deliberately overlooked it, is an important point in understanding the coolness of youth toward schools, and their view of them as hostile places.

Given the gap between the official culture of schools and that of youth who inhabit them, it is possible to see Carla's cartoons (apples talking to each other as they are being baked) as a sign of popular culture and her mood as resistance. Her inability or unwillingness to explain her work can be seen in the light of a refusal to participate in the overt culture of the school, and an air that seems to say, "Oh! what's the use. You wouldn't get it anyway, even if I told you." Writing about the increasing alienation of dislocated youth, Giroux (2000) argues passionately about the need to rethink the entire curriculum of schools that takes into account the "cultural transformation" that has occurred in recent times due to "massively new socializing contexts" that include large changes in demographics and the impact of the information age.

But Giroux's critique, like those of some other Critical theorists, while important and incisive, rarely gets down to the question of practice. In other words, while Giroux offers a powerful "language of critique," what is often missing is a microanalysis of the "language of possibility," to use Giroux's own terms. Hlebowitsh (2000) has remarked that there is an explicit admission of this among some Critical theorists themselves: "Giroux and Aronowitz have noted that the scholarship inspired by critical theory has a pessimistic character that tends to default on the commitment to curricular possibilities";

further, he also cites Giroux's observation that "radicals need to develop theories of practice rather than theories for practice" (91).

The above lacuna is met to a large extent by the Deleuzian approach, a thoroughgoing pragmatic one, that is concerned with experimentation at the level of everyday practice. To move to the Deleuzian perspective then, the first thing for the apprentice to note is that the pedagogic encounter itself is a theater of production of which the teacher-apprentice and student are co-producers. In this specific instance, the object of our attention, which is the production of a cartoon, is merely one participating series. Several regimes of signs enter into the production: + Teacher + Carla + Cartoon + Classroom +.... The and, and, and... shows the vertiginously proliferating circles of signs or heterogeneous series in the theater of production. This may be seen as a step in operationalizing the first component of the praxis I developed earlier—the adscension—that bids us to observe multiple regimes of signs that converge in the production or subjectivization of the dominant signifier. This immediately calls into question the interpretation that led to the unilateral positioning of the student as disengaged or recalcitrant. For such a conclusion can arise only by remaining a detached observer outside the theater of production. By semiotizing, we reject this hierarchical position, reentering the arena to release a variety of forms and substances of content and expression, no longer prey to one-sided and easy conclusions.

To put it differently, sensitized to the fact that the question of cartoons and the rest are themselves within the production of signs, and do not reflect independently existing essences, the teacher as a participant cannot remain external to their generation. In other words, the teacher becomes implicated in the production of the new series. This inevitably brings us to the point where we must deny dominant significations, and see the production as generating not faithful images but simulacra. That is, the cartoon is no longer a copy of the Idea of a cartoon, nor does it suggest a specific meaning, but a flickering matter-thought conglomerate that includes the observers. This in no way suggests a collapse of all genre into a primordial soup. On the contrary, it allows us to enter into a becoming together with the observed by breaking out of categories and boundaries. This shifts attention from the macro-perspective of subjects and interpretations to the micro-production of signs—to the gestures, language, semantics, speech acts, color, support, lines, body movements, random thoughts, irritation, irregular breathing, and to all other signs that arise in the tripartite encounter consisting of teacher, student and cartoon. We get away from the disease that Deleuze calls "interpretosis," or the desire to interpret as an uncovering of internal meaning. The original subjectivization that is the result of dominant signification is replaced by the production of simulacra.

Admittedly, it takes a considerable effort of thought to get away from the phenomenological subject, that is, to give up the transcendental viewpoint of the teacher and enter into a destratified plane wherein one has the same status as the signs themselves. But it becomes attractive once we see the pedagogical opportunities in doing so. The semiotization makes us lose the hard boundaries of our identities and the image of ourselves, which makes a considerable difference to the encounter. The entire scenario of Carla, the cartoons, and her uncooperative mood is now no longer wholly outside or independent of the teacher and is in a sense a *production* in which the teacher, who is the other end of the encounter, is inextricably implicated. As we semiotize ourselves, our reactions undergo a minor deterritorialization. This is the first step toward a Deleuzian empiricism, and the construction of the plane of immanence. It is also a first step toward establishing a more creative relationship with the Outside, as well as a way of making fuzzy one's notion of boundaries.

The second component of the analysis is the alloscension. Looking at the conversation, it is interesting to note that throughout the piece neither teacher nor student mention humor, which is what cartoons actually generate. They *produce* humor. They collapse different orders of concepts, or what Bateson (1991) has called "logical types" in a sudden precipitous move that brings about a schism. This is the transformational aspect, when sign regimes undergo change or mutate to produce new signs, new matter-thought conglomerates. Observation of these processes makes visible formations of micro-identities (Maturana and Varela, 1998), and makes our identities and boundaries more open and fluid. Also, the teacher's idea that cartoons must mean something undergoes a change once attention moves from meaning to experimentation and production of humor.

Thus, there is transformation of sign regimes. In the play of difference and repetition, differences repeat, but in the act of repetition become different. The transformational aspect helps us realize that we are constantly being produced even as we produce signs because there is no resting place; signs are constantly undergoing transformation, being taken over by new forces; new connectivities alter the significance of a sign, no longer signifying today what it signaled yesterday. This is important in the pedagogic relation—it foregrounds the continual minor transformations going on in our relationship to the distinctions with which we orient ourselves. Such reorientation, even if they be minor, result in a changed relationship of ourselves to ourselves, to knowledge, and to the student, and I argue that a different sensibility comes into play as a result of becoming aware of the flux that underlies the sign. It is an important step in the construction of the plane of immanence, where no firm line can be drawn between the experiencer and experience or observer and observed.

The third factor in the apprenticeship is the amnioscension. In the above example, humor as a deterritorializing, carnivalesque factor (Bakhtin, 1981) brings us to the diagrammatic or pragmatic part of our analysis. We have seen that signs contain singularities, or moments of becoming that begin prior to and spill beyond entities and subjectivities. Humor or laughter as packets of sensation spill out of the boundaries of personhood and are the reason why they are important in creating free spaces that are indeterminate, unregulated, even if momentarily, before being taken over by other forces.

These "free spaces," by loosening older arrangements, make room for new sensations to arise (Rajchman, 1998). In the case of Carla's cartoons, as a teacher one would have to refer to the production of humor, to the "anorganic vitality" of laughter which develops through minor crises in the sensory system. It is at this point, when teacher and student discover together their respective sensations in viewing, or otherwise reacting to a sign, that an infinitesimal moment of deterritorialization occurs. For "sensations are prior to forms and representations" (Rajchman, 1998, 7), and provide a space for embodied action or a becoming. Teacher and student occupy, if only for the briefest of intervals, an indeterminate space that is non-representational, and is diffractive rather than reflective, making an opening for new conversations. As we have noted earlier, the small interval is crucial for Deleuzian analysis, and in this case the space of the sensation construct becomes the smallest interval in which differential movements can be discerned. Varela (1992) argues that the temporal hinges that articulate enaction are rooted in the number of alternative microworlds that are activated in every situation. These alternatives are the source of both common sense and creativity in cognition. (17–18)

The alternative microworlds thus generated become sources of new curricular possibilities. To put it differently, since the sensation in the small interval is indeterminate and emergent, other configurations are always possible; that is, both the teacher as well as Carla's reactions may find new architectures in which to express themselves. Thus, affects become ways of generating new spaces that spin out of the cracks provided by the small interval.

Finally, there is the fourth component of the analysis—what I have called the anascension. The anascension is a meditation on the worldly sign that territorializes, that is, reduces signs to clichés and stereotypes. In this case, the teacher struggles with the student over the meaning of cartoons, that is, over signification, and thereby reifies it. The teacher remains with the representationalist ideas of what cartoons are rather than what they do, and thereby hollows out the sign—eliminating the possibilities of releasing, in resonance with the sign, the intensities that form alternative microworlds.

A similar exercise on another piece of data from the case study will further clarify the praxis. This time, I will turn the Deleuzian lens on a lengthy conversation I had with J.S. whom we met earlier:

K.R.: The other day you mentioned some difficulties you were having with one group of students. Could we discuss that a little bit?

J.S.: Yes. I was doing some slave narratives and they seemed not to be interested in it at all. That is kind of disappointing.

K.R.: Why do you feel they should be interested?

J.S.: Well, I certainly think these pieces are relevant. They are powerful and moving. It is also our history.

K.R.: What themes were you thinking of, precisely?

J.S.: Well, there are all kinds of issues of power and domination, and dehumanization...

K.R.: But on what plane are you casting them? I mean, there are the students, there is yourself, and there are these narratives. It seems to me that something else must happen for us to take our place within these narratives.

J.S.: You mean, I have to connect it to the students' experiences, is that what you are saying?

K.R.: Not exactly. But let's see if I can get this right. What is the sensation one might have when reading about extreme domination or dehumanization?

J.S.: Oh! Fear, hopelessness…and also anger.

K.R.: Okay. Let's take fear for the moment. Fear has a way of removing the barriers, don't you think? That could be emphasized.

J.S.: What barriers are you talking about?

K.R.: I mean fear is just fear, your fear is the same as my fear, fear has no label, the animal's fear is the same as my fear. The your and the mine come later, what do you think?

J.S.: I am not sure I get what you mean, but go on.

K.R.: I am basing this on my observation that fear is nothing special to me. Just like pain: neuromuscular discomfort. Therefore, it might be possible to construct the map of fear together. That's what I meant by taking our place in it.

J.S.: You mean like separate threads but coming together. Sounds weird. But I can see vaguely what you mean. You are talking about…like frequencies…

K.R.: Yeah, that's right, functioning together in a way that is neither you nor me nor anybody else, but at the same time all of us because we are made of these traits…I'm just trying to solve a problem.

J.S.: And you think we can do this with the students? [Laughs]

K.R.: I think we can, we have to be careful with this though. But what does this have to do with slave narratives and all that? Do you see any connection?

J.S.: I think you are asking if I can use specific feelings like anger or fear and create a certain resonance focusing on it. Involving students' own experiences of such feelings as part of the reading may be a good idea. (Interview with J.S. No. 2, and Follow-up Conversation)

In the above conversation, we are moving toward delineating what I am going to call a "diagram," a nonpersonal emanation such as a weather front that proceeds from resonating affects. Fear as an abstract diagrammatic deterritorializes, releases us from strata momentarily, forming a composite with others' fears. There is a becoming in fear or in any other trait that flees along virtual lines that have nothing to do with historical circumstances. It has to do with becoming. Capture it, enter into it, and we begin to develop a plane of immanence that ultimately changes the nature of fear itself, becoming something else. The same thing happens with desire. For Deleuze, desire precedes being, and is therefore immediately practical and political. It is practical precisely because it can actively participate in the drawing of the traits before the terms and relations are set, that is, before the boundaries of self and other are drawn. Fear and desire, reward and punishment have been used in the conventional curriculum as instruments of territorialization, that is, for emphasizing repetition and the thickening of strata through repetition which become authority structures. In a Deleuzian analysis, the same are now overturned to be used as tools of deterritorialization, as instruments of flight, of becoming.

To proceed with our analysis, let us look at the first component of our framework, the alloscension. The sign regime of the slave narratives in our example above was ostensibly bringing into play another set of signs seen by the teacher as disinterest and apathy — fluxes of expression and fluxes of content. But the important thing is to see the different regimes as mutually productive and playing into one another. That is, we do not look to see how to overcome the signs of apathy. Instead, we let the students' reactions or sign regimes flow into the theater of production. In other words, to the narratives of enslavement the teacher can invite the students to add their own feelings of being enslaved — to the teacher, the topic, the curriculum, or any other aspect — and dramatize the situation. Dramatizing the situation here would mean subjectivizing the feelings in different ways and connecting it to the topic of discussion. In this manner, there is a cross-fertilization between two regimes of signs that may give rise to yet others. Of course, the students may refuse to participate. But refusal brings forth an equally interesting regime of signs, evoking a new trope of resistance which is the transformational aspect — when signs mutate or undergo transformation and a new regime is born. The important thing here is to look at the signs as production, and keep oneself at the level of the sign.

Next, we must consider the amnioscension component. In the conversation above, I discuss with JS the possibility of detaching traits like fear or pain or helplessness and the possibility of constructing a map or an abstract diagram of traits or microworlds issuing from different bodies whereby our separate boundaries might undergo a minor destratification. In other words, experimentation with the generational and transformational aspects of signs can bring us to a point where we can see the possibility of traits emerging from beneath the signs and combining to form new multiplicities. This changes the image we have of ourselves as fixed entities; there is the possibility of a sudden crossing of boundaries when the traits become deterritorialized, that is, released from the composites or aggregates. This dissident flow or a minor current of disorientation unsettles our subjectivities and a rhizomatic moment can emerge. The rhizoid spaces thus generated create alternative microworlds for curricular exploration and are an enactment of a praxis that brings about embodied action rather than representation, and a play of difference rather than repetition.

In order to construct the diagrammatic, we have to pay attention to the smallest interval of interaction, in order that we may work our way past the dominant significations. We begin by paying attention to the small differences, inconsistencies, and gaps in our feelings, thoughts, and attitudes. In other words, subversion must be carried out at micro levels. In the small interval, Deleuze remarks:

We witness a transformation of substances, a dissolution of forms, a passage to the limit or flight from contours in favor of fluid forces or flows such that a body or a word does not end in a precise point. We witness the incorporeal power of that intense matter, the material power of that language. (Deleuze and Guattari, 1987, 129)

It is the small interval where incorporeal transformations occur, where catastrophic changes take place, where, according to Varela (1992), new microidentities emerge. An incorporeal transformation is thus "a passage to the limit" where change occurs as at the limit in differential calculus, where the units drop off, leaving us with the notion of pure change. We cease to end at a point or in the vicinity of a pre-given representational outline. In terms of practice, we observe and practice small changes in daily interaction; each observation of flux and indeterminacy constructs new awareness of embodied action in place of representationalist thought that leads to further changes in the ways we think and act. Bring about change in homeopathic doses, says Deleuze, not in grand, sweeping reforms. It means, in order to deterritorialize our boundaries and subjectivities, we have to observe the smallest variations in tone, language, gesture, thought, and movement that we produce in encounters. The more minute the observations the more effective it is. It is in the small interval that our traits and singularities begin to detach themselves from the composites, and we become aware of our collectivities. In this manner we escape identity.

Last, we have to consider the anascension component of the apprenticeship, or the empty sign. The empty or worldly sign captures intensities and domesticates them, thereby producing homologies. The sign regime of the slave narrative that J.S. brings into play can quickly turn into a cliché or acquire stereotypical features, with a corresponding loss of nuance, unless an investigation into the micropolitics of desire, subjection, and resistance makes each sign also into an action, a becoming in the lives of the actors that allows it to escape domestication. At the same time, within ourselves, we have to be watchful of the desire to dominate or be dominated—what Deleuze calls "microfascisms" in our constitution—that must be part of the forces that occupy the above signs and therefore must be kept under close scrutiny. The purpose of the whole exercise is to establish a different relationship with signs that allows fresh pedagogic possibilities, rather to enter the sign itself, and unleash a becoming that is a joint production in the learning encounter. In semioticizing ourselves thus, we become not reflective practitioners but diffractive ones.

This then is nomadic territory, a terrain populated by fluxes, flows, densities, and intensities, rather than things and outlines, and where new pedagogic possibilities arise as differentials and not as conjunctions; that is to say, as a result of attaining the limit in the boundary constructs and the consequent collapse of dominant significations, and not as representation and recognition. But we have to be cautious, for as Deleuze points out, stratification and destratification follow each other, and there is no such thing as being permanently situated in the nomadic, as we see below.

Some Methodological Precautions

In the following section, I will explain certain methodological precautions that we must observe in the apprenticeship and in creating a logic of multiplicities, that is, a logic of difference. It is necessary to pay attention to these so as to be able to approach the apprenticeship complexly, and without falling prey to simple dichotomies.

First, encounters continually generate signs which coagulate or decompose in multiple ways. To make sense of these continuous streams of signs is to invent a language. Deleuze has observed that there are many languages within a language. The reference here is not to a langue/parole (Saussure, 1959) distinction, nor is it an allusion to different registers or dialects within a language. Here, Deleuze is asking us to take responsibility for creating our own minor languages within major ones, languages of becoming without which we fall prey to the worldly sign. This acutely brings out the ethical responsibility in an encounter.

The second thing one must note is that deterritorialization and reterritorialization follow closely on each other's heels. To give an example, let us look at some excerpts from Maxine Greene's (1973) well-known book *Teacher as Stranger*. Greene rightly states the impossibility of establishing fixed criteria for interpreting cultural signs, but immediately afterward declares,

> Nevertheless nostalgia remains, and it is significant too. When a person thinks, for example, of *The Iliad*, with its heroic seekers after excellence...or of Shakespeare's plays, the magnitude of these works makes them seem truer, more intrinsically artistic than, say, Samuel Beckett's *Waiting for Godot*, Bernard Malamud's *The Fixer*, John Barth's *End of the Road* or Sylvia Plath's *Ariel*. (292)

After making a move away from attempts to totalize signs, Greene reterritorializes the ground she had opened up by claiming nostalgia as "significant," which takes us back to representationalist ground, and reestablishes hierarchy that requires ordering of signs according to intrinsic qualities or a Platonic interiority. Also, in the same essay Greene importantly notes the necessity of setting aside "everyday mode of apprehending" in interpreting signs, but then goes on to establish representational boundaries around a sign. Commenting on some specific pieces such as Picasso's *Guernica*, Greene articulates the manner in which these cannot be encountered, reassigning to the sign the role of the signifier:

> Encountering a work as art, the beholder is expected to set aside his everyday mode of apprehending. *Guernica* cannot be encountered as if it were a cartoon or a distorted rendering of an actual bombing (293).

But in a brief essay titled "Having an Idea in Cinema," Deleuze (1998) observes that art is not communication but purely an act of resistance. Without nitpicking, in the production of the sign, which is relational, an interdiction as above merely interferes with seeing the multiplicity of forces that occupy a sign. To say *Guernica* cannot be encountered as a cartoon is to reify both *Guernica* and the notion of the cartoon and deny their multiple ways of becoming in relation to the observer. For the cartoon is often an act of political resistance, and an effective one. In both the above examples, the apprentice must note the manner in which deterritorialization or destratification is quickly followed by reterritorialization. Dominant significations make their appearance after a momentary decentering.

The third thing to be aware of is that signs or phenomena are only partly sheathed in history, and therefore we must not make the error of overhistoricization. Chaos and complexity theory have amply demonstrated that a system's behavior cannot be wholly predicted from its history. Citing Nietzsche, Deleuze (1995) observes that "nothing important is ever free from a 'nonhistorical cloud.' What history grasps in an event is the way it's actualized in a particular set of circumstances; [but] the event's becoming is beyond the scope of history" (170). This can be illustrated by taking an example from embryology as follows.

An organism starts with a single cell, with a certain amount of genetic information. Through mitosis, the cell divides and multiplies, at all times the DNA is replicating itself. But then at one point groups of cells begin to differentiate, and one clump becomes the heart and another the liver. Nothing in the chemistry of the DNA itself can tell us how this happens, since all the cells had the *same initial conditions*. Historical determinism fails since historically all the cells started from the same cell. This is one of the enduring mysteries of cell biology.

There is no way to tell which group of cells would acquire certain morphological characteristics. Chance and contingency cannot explain the process of differentiation either. Something else is going on here that is nonhistorical and that is the product of complex interactions and emergent relations. This cautions us against overly historicizing phenomena, which can get us trapped in a particular set of expressions.

In the view that I take here, the sign's becoming is partly an atemporal flux that has no directionality but which appropriates all the tenses simultaneously. Its becoming is prior and parallel to its unfolding in time. It has the advantage of giving the teacher the space not only to think of her responses in learning encounters in terms of "Chronos," which has directionality, but also in terms of "Aion," which is timeless in the sense of maintaining no linear direction (Deleuze and Guattari, 1987). A meditation on this can give insight not only into the historicity of our subjectivities but also into the other dimension, that is, into the atemporal flux which is the outside of history—the "Untimely" of Nietzsche (1983). The awareness of the timely and the untimely together aid the apprentice of the sign to destratify and enter nomadic terrain.

Conclusion

There are no grand plans here, no overarching schemes for change, only a combat with pre-signifying forces to seize control of pathways of becoming, an awareness of the smallest interval in which transformation can take place, and a constant looking out for microfissures through which life leaks: "Imperceptible rupture, not signifying break" opens up these possibilities as stammerings, murmurs, decodings, and disorientations that start the movement toward a nomadology (Deleuze and Guattari, 1987, 24). To this end, the apprenticeship of the sign involves the realization of the following: a) every encounter generates signs; b) the meaning of a sign is not a given; c) signs are the result of production in which the observer and the observed are both implicated; d) one must forsake all tendency toward nostalgia in reading signs and treat them as a fresh problematic; e) signs are partly sheathed in a becoming that is outside history, that is, they are partly Chronos and partly Aion; f) one must hold at bay habitual responses while observing signs, the way one would in looking at a piece of art; g) signs must be freed time and again from old meanings and observed to see what they do and to whom; and h) the apprentice must be aware of their tendency to produce the worldly sign. A four-fold framework called the apprenticeship of the sign has been advanced as praxis toward such a transformation in thought, namely the adscension, the alloscension, the amnioscension, and the anascension.

The work is one of constructing a nomadic topos not toward any rosy future, but that is *anterior* to what is, and for which we have no mental representation precisely because it is an immanence. It is an *agencement* or deployment of intensities that is prior to phenomena— an intersection between teacher, student, and curriculum, between matter and thought, consisting of singularities and moments of the world that are not bound by subjectivity. For subjectivity is nothing but an effect of the great interweaving of materials, fluxes, and becomings. Using the notion of the a-signifying semiotic that allows us to access the differential forces occupying the sign, we construct a region that mainly consists of connectivities, lines, flows, and densities that are much more useful and flexible modes of thinking than conventional molar categories. Like a fractal entity, they generate, even proliferate, the space of becoming, creating new ways of relating to the world. This certainly involves a sustained movement of experimental engagement and awareness that facilitates travel beyond the habitual categories, something that can be accomplished by paying close attention to the nature of signs.

In other words, by means of such engagement, we adscend or slip laterally, past the signifying regimes that mold the intensities into existing strata, into a molecular level or the plane of becoming, shedding layers of deeply conditioned deployment of thought energies, and suddenly, perhaps for a split second, come free of rigid formations, before strata close in upon us again. It is important to note that deterritorialization is always partial and never a permanent state of affairs. Breakthroughs must give way again to molar formations or boundaries. That is to say, molecular states are constantly being returned to the molar.

But if it is the case that the molecular is constantly being recodified, then what might be the purpose of an undertaking such as the one above? Molecularity does not allude to any mysterious, mystical, or bizarre state of being that is permanent and irreversible. It is simply a newly developed sense of *being produced* even as we produce; in other words, it gives us a sense of duration or becoming rather than the staticity of a fixed identity. It allows us to deterritorialize, that is, to produce the hollows from where we can speak before sign regimes take over. It is the production of hollows or new spaces before these are eventually reterritorialized that is key to the praxis. Therefore, our task is incessantly to produce these hollows where the unthought can enter; rather, the hollow itself turns out to be the *unthought* of thought.

Further, in combating signifiers, we get a sense of the time dimension and what Deleuze calls the "virtual"; that is, in getting past the signifiers and order-words that cobble together our realities through structures of complex repetition, we come face-to-face with pure becoming that is nothing but an opening, an abyss. By means of the small moves of deterritorialization, we remain in what geologists call the "spallation zone," or the rim of a crater where the shock waves do not fully deterritorialize. In other words, we inhabit a limit where transforms of intensities and differentials occur and each minor move of destratification may be reinserted into the encounters to produce further autopoietic circles of causality, amplifying successive rounds. But this difficult line of work necessitates a more rigorous exploration of affect, since a key move in the reconstellation of sense data into rhizoid space is to "free the trait," or to loosen the singularities or microidentities that are nothing other than affects — the blocks of intensities and fields of flux beneath our constituted selves. This is the discussion that follows in the next chapter.

But before that, let me once again clarify that a curriculum of intensities does not mean launching into some mindless movement of unreason. And although it bears tireless repetition from the margins of modernist practices that "our emotions enter legitimately and constitutively" into all formal operations including scientific activity, and that we "exist" only as "bodynodes of a dynamic intercrossing of discourses and emotions" (Maturana, 1990, 25–27), my effort here is directed more toward a specificity. It has to do with the fact that

It is the differentiation of what exists that is contributed by the observer's *imagination*, since, with the support of the specification of distinctions an immensely rich structure of combinations can be obtained." (Luhmann, 1990, 69) (emphasis added)

In other words, the worlds that we build depend on the quality and range of distinctions that we can produce or make available, which, in turn, depend on the imagination.

But here again, I want to pin down imagination to something more than the garden variety understanding of it as giving free reign to the "mental" production of images and of representation. I wish to be able to regard imagination in the present context in terms of what we have seen in Maturana and Varela (1998) as a "readiness for action" at the level of the microphysics of our constitution as we move between realms and discourses. Imagination is thus the gap between two concrete moments, grasping which we begin to live "according to a production, a productivity, a potency, in terms of causes and effects" (Deleuze, 1988a, 3). In other words, affect as imagination is pure potency, appearing at the limit where the virtual becomes the actual. It is thus that intensity and affect become a matter of life and death, and the worlds we construct depend on the level and extent of experimentation that we are prepared to conduct upon them. It happens when we are able and willing to stake our entire being behind every utterance.

Second, commenting on the Oedipal processes at work in the formation of molar categories, Massumi (1992) writes incisively about the family's overcoding role within Capitalism that gives a jolt to popular notions:

> A body does not grow up sheltered from society, enclosed in the family that feeds it. Rather, the family opens the door to society's feeding itself off [the body]. The family is a device for the capture of body potential by social forces of domination dedicated to the vampiric extraction of surplus value. (81)

It is easy to see how the term "family" can be replaced in the above analysis by teachers and the education system in general that work within this process of "vampiric extraction of surplus value," which is nothing other than a recuperation of affect under heavily skewed power relations. For the metaphorics of vampirism is nothing if not the illegitimate siphoning off and concentration of affect.

From this perspective, the redistribution of affect can only take place if we grapple with the intensities produced in a learning encounter prior to their being overcoded and assigned to a molar category or subsumed under a signifier system. Our battle has been to find ways of releasing precisely these affects that are continuously being siphoned off and overcoded, that is, eclipsed from sight, and therefore robbed of their potential for contributing to curriculum by dominant sign systems. The apprenticeship is such an anti-vampiric effort that proceeds by the awareness of codification processes that are at work. The release of intensities from their codification under the despotic signifiers allows for a smooth space to emerge in which the categories are less important than the emergence of multiplicities. This does not mean, however, that multiplicities are not distinguishable from one another, only

> not at all in the same manner as forms and the terms in which these are incarnated. They are objectively made and unmade according to the conditions that determine their fluent synthesis. (Deleuze, 1994, 187)

In other words, multiplicities are continually differentiating but without taking any final determinate forms. This is vitally important from a pedagogic angle since it urges us to give up, for instance, the notion of the teacher as a determinate being. Instead, we learn to look in terms of the fluctuating fields of habits, affects, and ideas that are in continual flux. The labor that remains before us is to take a closer look at affect in order to understand this dynamic relationship and the formation of the field of composition.

Notes

1. In the *Logic of Sense*, Deleuze writes that in Plato, the simulacrum implies unmanageable "dimensions, depths, and distances that the observer cannot master." In other words, Plato suspects the uncontrollable and rebellious nature of the forces at play, and in order to "impose a limit" on this limitless becoming, attempts "to shut it up in a cavern," that is, in the dungeons of identity (258). Deleuze argues that this "unformed chaos" that Plato considers subversive is

precisely the power of affirmation that allows us to break the chains of identity and representation.

2. To be sure, as Massumi (1992) points out, the point of departure is always a molarized situation, because the choices themselves are expressed in molar terms, but the process of transformation itself is not molar.

3. Cell differentiation is a good case in point. Cells starting from the same initial conditions break symmetry at a point and become differentiated into specific tissue. The symmetry breaking cannot be explained through either biology, mathematics, information science or any other theory in isolation. The process itself exceeds all of these and can be thought of as a cutting edge of complexity in which the usual distinctions between matter and thought, or the abstract and the concrete, vanish.

Chapter 5

Becoming Nomad

Affects aren't feelings, they are becomings that spill over beyond whoever lives
through them.   —— Gilles Deleuze, *Negotiations*

A significant problem never loses its problematicity despite having
numerous solutions, since it persists in its very solutions, which it
spawned and from which it must also differ. To put it differently,
problems are not problematic because of the limitations of the state of
our empirical knowledge, but the "problematic" is precisely "a state
of the world" (Deleuze, 1994, 280). Let us recall that one of the
problems that I outlined in the beginning was the problem of affect—
in particular, stress—in novice teachers. The problem of stress is not a
problem one can "solve," due to its complex multiplicity, although
one can have numerous local solutions. But it alerts us to what
Deleuze calls the "reality of the virtual" (280). That is, it signals the set
of abstract differential relations or series of contractions and
contemplations that order intensities into proximate arrangements.
Seen in this manner, stress becomes, simply, different distributions of
"mobile singularities" or blocks of intensities and their formations
that we have discussed earlier. Such a redescription is important for
establishing the link between stress, affect, and curriculum, as also the
relevance of its discussion here. The link is in the virtual. To remind
ourselves, the virtual is not essence or any ideal state, nor is it virtual
reality. It is simply the potential for differentiating such as in the case
of the differentiating egg that we saw earlier. It is also certainly not
the possible: "whereas the possible is the mode of identity of concepts

within representation, the virtual is the modality of the differential" (Deleuze, 1994, 279). It is, in a sense, pure becoming that escapes determination and yet determines.

In the introduction and chapter 3, I observed that a restrictive and limiting view of curriculum and learning that came out of representationalist conceptions created resentment and stress in teachers who unfortunately sought resemblance and identity in the highly differentiated urban conditions of the school. In the language of our analysis, the affective investments were tied to certain notions of becoming, to particular resonances. Given that our commitment is to find ways of looking, thinking, and experimenting that allow us to escape the representationalist ground and enter a more nomadic terrain that can deal with irregular and divergent spaces, we have to find new pathways of distributing affect that lead away from stressful configurations. To this end, we have to continue our work of mapping or conceptualization, which, as Britzman and Dippo (1998) point out, is

> not just about articulating ideas but also about making sense about the myriad feelings one has about ideas. Conceptualization brings together affect and cognition precisely because structures of meaning cannot be divorced from structures of feeling, investments, and desires. (22)

Thus, a concept is not just an intellectual notion, a product of Cartesian reason; it has woven into it affective qualities at the same time. How we construct something conceptually is inextricably linked with our structures of investments, feelings, and desires. Conceptualization is a hybrid of thought, emotion, and desire. Therefore, reconceptualization must also affect stress. In other words, I am suggesting that a change in the conceptual structure in which one is immured can significantly influence affective states and thereby positively affect stress. But what is more important from the Deleuzian perspective is the possibility of *producing* affect, a unique contribution that goes beyond containment of negative affect to the generative. It is this positivity of affect that can lead us into new becomings. But before we go into the question of stress from a Deleuzian perspective, let us first very briefly look at the problem of teacher stress as portrayed in mainstream education literature, mainly in order to identify the major assumptions of the analyses.

Stress and Identity

Stress is an aspect in the becoming and the *un*becoming of a teacher that is of serious concern according to all available indices (Byrne 1998). Abel and Sewell (1999) observe that prolonged stress associated with the gradual erosion of important technical, psychological, and social resources results in burnout. Maslach (1993) has suggested that burnout among individuals who do "people work" tends to be multidimensional, composed of emotional exhaustion, depersonal-ization, and reduced personal accomplishment. Emotional exhaustion includes increased feelings of depleted emotional resources and feelings of not being able to provide oneself to others at a psychological level. Depersonalization occurs when an individual develops negative attitudes toward students because of depleted emotional resources. Abel and Sewell (1999) emphasize the need for effective coping strategies targeting sources of stress.

The existing literature recognizes that relationships with pupils have been the most important source of stress for teachers (Friedman 1995), and several studies have also indicated that poor student attitude is consistently a predictor, if not the best predictor, of teacher stress (Borg and Riding, 1993; Boyle et al., 1995). Other major sources of stress identified by teachers have been administrative apathy and work overload. A review of the literature also reveals that the organizational approaches which have been used in schools to combat burnout have been managerial in style and technique (Boice, 1993). These include the skills of managing time, communicating, planning leisure time, and methods of reducing psychological stress. Finally, the literature states that in-service programs and workshops devoted to various forms of relaxation training, such as visualization, quieting reflexes, autogenics, and biofeedback, often provide renewal techniques for the burnt-out teacher

In all this, what is important to note is the way stress is taken to be an attribute of the teacher as a self-enclosed entity. Although it is recognized that teacher-student relations are a major contributor to stress, the relationality itself is considered as something external to the phenomenon. The second thing to note is that the nature of the actions proposed in order to "combat" or eliminate stress and burnout is of the order of restoration of an original stress-free identity. That is, they presuppose an original representational wholeness. Each of these, ranging from positive feedback to stress reduction training, from meditation to managerial techniques, is individualistic and therefore deals with one end of the problem, ignoring the relationality of the issue, or the *encounter*. Stress arises in an encounter, although its effects may be more readily visible in the body of the teacher. In the dialectical mode of analyzing the problem, the vital two-way relationality of the encounter gets eclipsed. The mainstream literature thus leans on a one-sided analysis of the problem, seeing stress as a problematic of a certain kind of depletion of self.

From the above perspective, stress results in the perception that one is no longer fully oneself, that is, in a sense of diminished powers of being and acting. Therefore, stress may also be described as a kind of fragmentation of identity due to the impact of several external forces. Now, identity, or being oneself, in the language of our analysis, can only arise by being identical, or as the occurrence of pure resemblance *without difference*; that is, we feel ourselves to be the *same* individual over time and through myriad experiences. In other words, identity must come out of *perfect repetition*. Only if matter or the Cogito repeats itself perfectly, *ad infinitum,* can there be the sense of the identical, or the Same. So also in Freudian psychoanalysis, repetition appears as foundational, and occurs through a schema of opposition and the mechanics of repression, repeating also in the model of the death instinct.

Rethinking Repetition
We have seen earlier that the order of concept is closely linked with the order of affect, and consequently, if we can show that the basic conceptual model which is subsumed by stress-related affective distributions are problematic, and identify the nature of the difficulties therein, we will be in a position to reconsider stress. In this case, the first step in our analysis will be to show that pure repetition or perfect resemblance is impossible. That is to say, pure repetition is perfectly illusory. It means that repetition is not possible without difference, nothing more, nothing less. The consequences of this will become clear as we proceed, but primarily, by breaking out of the illusion of pure repetition or identity we can hope to lay the ground

for a different order of reconstitution. In order to do this, we will first have to delve into some relatively dense theory that is unavoidable for grasping Deleuze's work.

First, repetition occurs when things are distinguished in numbers, in space and time, while apparently their *concept remains the same*. Two identical pencils are said to be repetitions of the same concept. In other words, repetition is difference without a concept. Since the pencils are separated in space and time, there is a difference, but this difference is external to the concept since they are not seen to differ in concept. So there is a difference without there being a difference, and "repetition is represented outside the concept...*but always with the presupposition of an identical concept*" (Deleuze, 1994, 270). This shows the first distortion in thinking about repetition as pure resemblance.

Second, the model of representation in which repetition occurs "suppresses the thickness in which repetition unfolds" (271). The numerical multiplicity, in the case of the above example of pencils, does not occur in empty nothingness but within strata of space and time and matter. To think repetition therefore presupposes a subjective thinker. That is to say, it can only be "understood in relation to a thought identity...with the result that repetition remains a concept of reflection... for a spectator who remains extrinsic" (272). Therefore, there is a hidden observer present in the notion of repetition in whom is played out the game of repetition. But the subject implies all manner of mediating influences including memory and thought that introduce difference.

Third, Deleuze writes, "The Same would never leave itself to be distributed across several 'equivalents'...if difference were not displacing itself and disguising itself in this same" (290). There must necessarily be an external force that would transport the sameness to numerical multiplicities, and this force is difference. Therefore, we see repetition as a kind of disguising and a displacement that attempts to deny the fact that repetition is really a complex phenomenon that has layers and layers within it separated by difference. And this "evasive in-betweenness of expression's emerging into and continuing through a cluttered world is why it is never 'autonomous' in the sense of being a separate entity" (Massumi, 2002, xxix). Therefore, repetition cannot succeed in returning the Same:

The Negative does not return. The Identical does not return. The

Same and the Similar do not return. Only affirmation returns — in other words, the Different, the Dissimilar. (299)

What returns is affirmation in the form of swirling singularities or "crowned anarchies" that are endless variations of variations. In other words, what returns are simulacra: "Simulacra are those systems in which different relates to different *by means of* difference itself...[We] find in these systems no *prior identity*, no *internal resemblance*." (299)

Stress and the Simulacrum
In keeping with the above analysis therefore, the first step in dealing with stress is to understand ourselves not as identities that return every day, day after day, but as "crowned anarchies" or systems of simulacra in which only affirmation returns as a differential. This is basic to a Deleuzian approach that attempts to bring about a change in the image of thought, that aims to have thought without an image that is prior to it, and thereby reaches what Deleuze calls the "genitality" of thought. Reaching the genitality of thought means to come into contact with the sea of excess contractions or expressions that go beyond all molar identities. We then carry with us not just a prior identity thrust upon us by the idea of a false return, an obligation to be the same, but a becoming-intense by the realizing of all the uncaptured excess that lies beyond strata. In this way we encounter "a world which cannot be assimilated to everyday banality...but one in which resonates the true nature of that profound groundlessness which surrounds representation" (277). That is to say, we enter every encounter not as grounded beings with fixed identities, but with the groundlessness and affirmation of the simulacra. It is the groundlessness that is key to the excess that is generated around any determination:

Expression's moving-through is non-consciously inflected in the body by a cascade of repeated determinations, no sooner follow-ed by passings into the gaps of systemic indeterminacy between its strata. The body's layered processing injects as much chance inflection as it does serial definition. (Massumi, 2002, xxx)

This systemic indeterminacy gives rise to a creative uncertainty that continually results in new determinations or inflections: It is the production of the simulacrum rather than identity. Therefore, a necessary shift in thought, one that is required if we are to grapple with stress and affect without falling into false negativities, is to think in terms of the simulacra. But one more step remains: For the purpose of our analysis, we have to be able to formulate the notion of stress in terms of the Deleuzian notion of affect, which is explained below.

Affect as Transition

For Deleuze (1988a), affects are movements from one state to another, "transitions, passages that are experienced, durations through which we pass" to an enhanced or diminished sense of being. These "continual variations" that create a movement in time from a "preceding state towards the next state" are called affects. That is to say, affects are modifications that act upon previous modifications, leaving corporeal traces which involve both "the nature of the affecting body and the affected body." Further, affects are "purely *transitive*, and not indicative or representative, since [they are] experienced in a lived duration that involves the difference between two states" (48–49).

In other words, affects are transitions or *differences* between states produced in relationship, and if we ask about the nature of these differences, we cannot get a representational interpretation precisely because it is experienced as a transition *between* states. "But the idea which constitutes the form of the affect affirms of the body something which involves more or less of reality than before" (Spinoza cited in Deleuze, 1988a, 49). This means that although we cannot translate the differential into representational terms, its effect is felt as an expansion or diminution of our "mode" of being, that is, our capacity to be affected and to act.

To put it simply then, affect is something which either increases or decreases our power to be affected, and since it is always relational, it produces new modes from preceding states that affect all parts of the relation, that is, all bodies that enter into the relation.[1] So when we say a body is affected, we mean that a certain mode encounters another mode and enters into a composition with it, thereby increasing or diminishing its "power of acting or force of existing" (Deleuze, 1988a, 50). Accordingly, stress can be thought of as negative affect, a certain transitional moment in the composition of bodies.

Let us for a moment return to the apprenticeship and its four components. The reader will note that the main thrust of the experiment was to return expression to the indeterminate by closely examining sign systems that encode the forces of expression or the comings-to-be.[2] For processes carry much greater potential than signs could possibly reflect, and sign regimes, by giving too much definition to the processes, negate the excess. The apprenticeship attempts to return the determinate endings to the indeterminate, attempting thereby to reinsert the determinate wholes back into the sea of becoming. It is also by means of such an apprenticeship that we locate ourselves in that space of transition between states, an indeterminate region, whereby we can reconnect to the potentialities and mobile singularities. We are now ready to look at some case data to see how this reconceptualization can help in the pedagogic encounter.

Analysis of Case Data

Let us look at the following example from the case study. I talked to L.S. who revealed an unusual angle to the problem of stress.

K.R.: Could you talk about some specific things, behaviors, attitudes that have been stressful for you since you came here.
L.S.: Oh, where shall I start! There are several things but I have this feeling that some of the students either want to push you up or bring you down. And that is one. Do you know what I mean?
K.R.: I am not sure if I followed you. Could you please elaborate?
L.S.: Well, I think it is a status thing. Either you must have status in their eyes or they ignore you. I have spoken to some others and they have similar feelings.
K.R.: Oh I see. But how does one acquire status?
L.S.: Oh, it could be many things. You may come in with a certain status for various reasons, or it could be the way other staff treat you, the way they look at you. It could be the subject you teach.
K.R.: And in what ways does this affect you?
L.S.: It interferes with the way you function as a teacher; there is an invisible frame around you. And the status determines whether students pay any attention to you or not. And also you feel crowded, less room to maneuver.
K.R.: Is this entirely beyond the control of the teacher?

L.S.: I think a large part of it comes out of certain expectations. (Interview with L.S. No.2)

L.S. sees the problem of stress as vitally related to the issue of status, to the way one is seen in the other's world, to how one is positioned, in other words, in terms of her identity. Thus, feelings of indifference or student apathy that cause stress are directly related to social images of who we are.

L.S. is engaged in a mental effort of representation, one that attempts to create a coherent map of her relations *in advance* and thereby brings forth a compelling narrative-world that is negative and stressful. The conceptual shift that is to be made here is to realize that these relations are not positivities but emergent differentials, and the affects they trigger are fields of flux. In other words, stress is not a state but a sensation that arises in transiting between states. The effort of the apprentice is to remain in this space of transition. The causal claim that "I am stressed due to..." is an abstraction whose actual embodied action needs to be studied, for as Varela (1992) has pointed out, "cognitive intelligence resides only in its embodiment" (59). What all this amounts to is a shift in attention from overarching descriptors such as stress to the planes of fracture and microintervals produced by tectonic shifts wherein the nameless enactive moment actually emerges, and which contains generative possibilities. Such a praxis can be achieved by becoming aware of the transitional moments of affective states. The excitement begins once one takes hold of this theater of production and the structures within it (Massumi, 1992, 67) and through careful observation and experimentation discovers what Deleuze calls the possibilities of the virtual, and what Varela (1992) would call "neural narratives" of the imagination. That is to say, one becomes situated in the in-between-ness of the transitive that moves not along predetermined lines, but along the virtual and therefore has a certain flexibility and spontaneity.

The above points may be further clarified by looking at another piece of data from the case study and the analysis that follows. In this case, E, an older teacher, expresses her fears and her stressful condition:

E: I think my real stress has come about because of working with students and getting closely connected to their problems for a long time. I love the students and many of the kids come in and tell me what is going on. Sometimes listening to them can be exhausting. I find myself jumping in wanting to act and do something to change what is going on in their lives. I feel very strongly about this, and this causes me a lot of stress. I go to their homes, I contacted T by going to her house to tell her she has to be in school to meet the psychologist the next day if she wanted a referral from her. But her home conditions overwhelmed me. I found I could not teach after that for a while. Over time, this has become very depressing for me. How does one listen to the depressing stories of kids' lives and not get depressed oneself? But maybe depression is not the word. I do not know my own feelings anymore. That is my question. I have been working with these kids and their personal problems so closely and I have felt recently that I cannot continue here anymore because I am too fragile now. (Interview with E No.2)

Here we see the case of a teacher who is close to what she feels as a breakdown in her emotional well-being due to stress. The pressure of consistent close interactions has opened up lines of fracture, but it is these lines of break or affective rupture that offer possibilities of fresh investigation within pedagogy. To quote Britzman (1998):

[A] more useful way to think about feelings requires attention to what it is that structures the ways in which feelings are imagined. [Therefore] pedagogy might provoke the strange study of where feelings break down...pedagogy might become curious about what conceptual orders have to do with affectivity. (84)

By bringing the conceptual structure we have developed to bear on where feelings break down, we can move along a different pathway. According to Varela (1992), where feelings break down is precisely where "the concrete is born" (11). In other words, the performative takes place in between states; critical transitional moments open up gaps in our "molar identities" or apparent continuity and inspire a certain force, a freedom of observation and action due to the indeterminacy inherent in the situation. Even more emphatically, Varela (1992) notes that "it is the breakdowns, the hinges that articulate microworlds, that are the source of...the creative side of living cognition" (11). In Deleuzian terms, schisis leads to leakages and the consequent regaining of a degree of "molecularity"; it acts to remove the organism from its normal habitat of sameness and identity to a *becoming-other* or a continually differentiating space where a degree of spontaneous generation can occur. In other words, "breakdowns," or critical moments of transition, are generative moments when something new might happen. In such a praxis, concept, percept, and affect act together to produce the observation of a microidentity or singularity that is

> a mode of individuation very different from that of a person, subject, thing, or substance. They consist entirely of relations of movement and rest, capacities to affect and be affected. (Deleuze and Guattari, 1987, 261)

These becomings that spill out of determinate boundaries form modes of enactive perception. E's condition inadvertently exhibits such a becoming. The temporary absence of boundary or molecularity that E experiences, rather than diminishing her capacities to be and to act, can actually enhance it once she learns to look in terms of transitions and the simulacra or microidentities, and fully embraces the field of entanglement, giving up the struggle to maintain transcendent categories. In other words, the state of vulnerability that E epitomizes is an entry to a multiplicity. Such an operation "opens a space in the grid of identities those categories delineate, inventing new trajectories, new circuits of response, unheard-of futures...and maps out a whole new virtual landscape" (Massumi, 1992, 101). By deliberately cultivating this field through the observation of transitions, we enter praxis.

Further, E says she does not know her feelings anymore, revealing an indeterminate state where E can only have a sense of her fragility. It is the careful direction of such moments of "schisis," aided by a conceptual deterritorialization, that leads to the opening of a

> fractal abyss where [earlier] there was only a hyphen between stimulus and response, and canned reaction. The body's zone of indeterminacy...widen[s] beyond measure. This increase in the body's degrees of freedom is called "imagination." Imagination

takes the body not as an "object" but as a realm of virtuality...as a site for superabstract invention. (Massumi, 1992, 100)

Without the benefit of an experimentation of the kind outlined in the apprenticeship to direct her deterritorialization, E unfortunately has moved toward a diminished state of powers of acting and being. I suggest that, with an experimental awareness of the process of releasing affects from signifiers and the corresponding relative deterritorialization, teachers can turn such affective moments to productive use and redirect them into the forming of multiplicities. That is, they can engage in generating new microintensities or simulacra that can reconfigure stress into a positivity.

To recount then, in Deleuzian-Spinozian terms, stress can be redescribed as transitional states in the combination of bodies that lead to negative consequences. Given the concept-affect correspondence, it leads to the position that stress or a decrease in powers of acting and being can be a consequence of the habit of maintaining transcendent categories. This can be reversed by affective formations that recombine intensities according to a different schema. In the above example, E says that her condition is the result of "being too closely connected" to the kids and their problems. But these categories are external to the experience of stress itself. In other words, these categories do not preexist on the plane of affect; instead, what *is*, is the experience of intensity and entanglement. A Deleuzian praxis can help E to widen her repertoire of responses.

However, no one knows at the outset the affects of which the body is capable. Therefore, "it is a long affair of experimentation, requiring a lasting prudence" that is necessary to enter a widening range of responses, and invent the necessary neural narratives for those new becomings (Deleuze, 1988a, 124). Below is a piece of case data that exhibits possibilities of pedagogic experimentation:

J.S. has been teaching slave narratives in his literature class. It is something he feels passionate about but he is disturbed by his students' lack of response to these powerful accounts. Over the term J.S.'s anxiety has risen over the apathy and the indifference of the students. He admits to feeling increasingly stressed. But something has happened that has begun to turn things around. J.S. said, after a while he could see the students' point of view. He

shared the students' sense of frustration. As soon as that happened, the character of his negative emotions began to change.
(Field Note No.16)

From thinking about stress from a unilateral perspective, J.S. seemed
to have been moved to appreciate the encounter. I follow up this
issue with J.S.:

J.S.: At this point I realized that I have to change my orientation,
that I had certain fixed ideas about what they should be learning
and how.
K.R.: What about the sense of frustration you spoke about earlier?
J.S.: There's less of that now, that's one result of the change, I
began to feel less of it personally.
K.R.: Why do you think that happened?
J.S.: I think it happened one day when I had hit the bottom. I
asked myself what was I opposing. I hadn't taken into account
student frustrations seriously up until that point. Since then I
have begun to change some things.
K.R.: You mean there is no frustration now?
J.S.: No, but it does not have the emphasis on myself anymore. I
am doing things differently now. (Interview with J.S. No.2)

Earlier, J.S. had not taken into account students' affects and
frustrations. In other words, their affects were not allowed to enter
into a relationship with the material. Later, that changes; proceeding
in this manner, with careful experimentation, J.S. can reenter the
multiplicity beyond determinate formulations, that is, a degree of
molecularity that "evoke[s] an indeterminate number of pragmatic
responses" (Massumi, 1992, 100). The line of thought that was
occupied by personal stress is taken beyond itself and remapped onto
a different set of conceptual coordinates. Taken further, by means of a
reconceptualization of the kind I have suggested here, it could help
J.S. to enter a more fertile zone of existential openings.

Conclusion
Thus, in a given encounter, careful observation and cautious
experimentation will reveal the scope of affectivities. This has
significant consequences for the problem of stress. For it means that

certain modes and images of thought—thought invested in maintaining molar categories—are likely to induce stress in the pedagogical situation. A change in the image of thought helps us escape the negativities and produce simulacra. The effort is to somehow take charge of that production, to seize the means of constructing the patchwork of the plane of immanence in which we ourselves become the efficient cause, the *producer*. This is the central difference between, say, a social psychology approach to stress and the Deleuzian approach. Deleuze discusses and shows us the possibility of the *production of affect*.

In our analysis, the production begins when we realize, by means of the apprenticeship, that our molar categories are built from "small domains composed of microworlds and microidentities" (Varela, 1992, 18), the "unruly interactions" and not totalizing integration between whom give rise to a cognitive moment. The realization of these microidentities or multiplicities that link up with other microaffects affords a self-seeding, and with that the possibility of moving from effect to cause, or from stress to productivity, and is capable of dealing with the problem of stress and affect in a singularly comprehensive way. In other words, it repotentializes the body into becoming an event and helps to circumvent habit:

> Habit is the body's defence against shocks of expression. It 'recognizes' every arriving perception as being 'like' an impulse the body has already integrated as a functional life content. It contains potential with resemblance....The resemblance is in the redundancy of response...The sameness of the response depends precisely on disregarding the singular contours of the arriving impulse: dismissing its potentially tortuous anomalies as func-tionally insignificant. (Massumi, 1992, xxxi)

The body being composed of multiple layers of strata is not often predisposed to think but to operate out of habit. Much of what we have discussed is an attempt to dislodge from the old habits of thought in which the body becomes frozen. To dislodge here means to see thought itself as an event, and not as a representation of an event, that is, not in terms of another reification. This is the transformative power of thought without an image.

But, how do we connect this to the affect of the everyday work in classrooms? An example may be useful here. Let us consider Samuel Beckett's *Waiting for Godot*. One plausible theme of the play is existential boredom of an extreme kind. But as Deleuze has pointed out, neither the actors nor the dialogue is boring, nor is the reader bored. Here we see the movement of pure affect as boredom without boring anybody. Instead, the very affect—boredom—is detached from molar identities and carefully experimented with, looked at from various angles. Experimenting with boredom in this manner is never boring, but quite the opposite. It dehabituates us from thinking about boredom as an attribute of a subject. Similar experimentation with pure affect may be found in the writings of Virginia Woolf and Herman Melville, among others. Such experimentation leads to a fundamental change in the image of thought, or rather, it opens us up to thought itself as an event.

In other words, when we sense that affects are singularities that exceed the expressions within habit, we can open ourselves to that excess that exceeds the designations and significations of habitual thinking, and begin to live as an aspect of a dynamic limit, or a metastable entity (Deleuze, 1990b, 104). Pushed beyond a critical threshold, affects get knocked out of their habitual orbital paths that collectively produce the illusion of enduring categories, and instead appear as openings, tiny abysses. We no longer remain passively bound to affects through sentiment, but instead become active participants in their production by entering the very zone of that production.

But a doubt is thrown in our midst. Is this not what Kane succeeds in doing in Orson Welles' great film *Citizen Kane*? Does not Charlie Kane pursue, Ahab-like, his affect, his "Rosebud," the obscure object of his desire to the ends of the earth? (Beller, 1998, 90) And in that process, does Kane not become an instance of pure desire strung out into so many singularities of the kind I have been suggesting? While it is true that Kane unmoors himself in the pursuit of what remains the unthought within the film, he remains within the trap of the signified, his childhood sled "Rosebud" that is emblematic of the Oedipal separation that is forever out of his grasp. As we have noted earlier, movements within Capital and other forms of State logic also deterritorialize, but these are immediately followed by new kinds of stratification that quickly siphon off the affective energies thus released. Kane's deterritorialization is simultaneously a reterritorialization, as it is recuperated within his desperate logic of accumulation and the Oedipalized search for an absolute signified. I have also said earlier that in freeing signs from despotic regimes and the affective energies bound up with them, one must be cautious about precisely this recodification.

But what precautions are available against such doubling back? In order to answer that question, the map must now be briefly extended beyond the work of the apprenticeship, beyond the freeing up of desire or intensities, and into a confrontation with what Deleuze has called the "line of the Outside," or to a face-off with thought itself. In the concluding section, I shall discuss this phenomenon.

Notes

1. When we say bodies, we do not necessarily mean whole entities. In the present framework, even an optically sensitive surface that contracts into it a ray of light is a body; it is what Guattari has called a "part-subject" or what Maturana and Varela have described as "microidentities." A larger body, such as a human body, is simply an assembly of these part-subjects or microidentities.

2. Expression here refers to the theory and ontology of Expressionism, that is, to the genesis of forms and structures in which forces take definition. It is not to be confused with linguistic expression, just as signs must not be thought here in terms only of language.

Conclusion

The Line of the Outside

The technocrat is the natural friend of the dictator—computers and dictatorship; but the revolutionary lives in the gap which separates technical progress from social totality, and inscribes there his dream of permanent revolution. This dream, therefore, is itself action, and an effective menace to all established order; it renders possible what it dreams about. — Gilles Deleuze, *The Logic of Sense*

We started by looking at some problems that surfaced in the case study—the difficulties novice teachers faced in a highly differentiated environment where they sought similarity and resemblance and correspondence with mainstream attitudes toward schooling. The urban school described in the case offered pedagogical possibilities more in the way of irregular, uncertain, and in-between spaces that were closer to the "leaky" needs of urban youth who attended the school. While the dynamics of school relations at this particular site continually resisted being confined to the staid space of representation and resemblance, and cried out for a different kind of mapping that would better articulate the possibilities therein, the data showed that the teachers, not conceptually prepared to deal with difference as a positivity, were often unable to take advantage of these in-between spaces for making pedagogical moves. Something substantial always leaked—the school leaked out of "State" space in serious ways; few in the district office understood what it was doing; the staff leaked out of contractual space in attempting to make school somehow relevant to youth with different needs within an unresponsive and wooden state system; the students spilled out of the formal curriculum and onto wider social spaces, and the curriculum moved out of the classroom and was designed to be full of different lines of flight through which students, many of whom would otherwise have dropped out, could find escape routes to different becomings not anticipated within the district's official curriculum.

The case study illustrated the difficulty beginning teachers had in constructing and practicing a contextually relevant pedagogy in this highly differentiated urban space; the tendency was to reduce difference to identity, to the established, conventional mode of curricular practices from which the school had attempted to escape in the first place. It resulted in a strong pull toward the center. Therefore, my theoretical intervention in the way of offering theory as praxis was to find a way to make teachers aware of the constructivist possibilities of positive difference. The effort was to help teachers locate themselves in the flow of a praxis by means of which to move to an alternate conception of curriculum than the representationalist one. This praxis was worked out within the frame of a Deleuzian empiricism that insists that reality is cocausal and not a given, but rather an "eternally recommenced creation" (Massumi, 1992, 53) through reciprocal presupposition or mutual determination. The basis of this lay in the differential nature of Deleuzian eco-ontology.

Following Spinoza and Hume, Deleuze considers all phenomena to be nonidentical, provisional, multiplicitous, and a product of difference. Entities do not belong to categories; it is the categories that are abstracted from the multitudes. In considering the case study in this light, we saw the case data resonate with the notion of multiplicity and rhizomatics. Realizing our multiplicities is a first step toward breaking down identitarian ways of thinking, and releasing the power of difference. It is not a mere question of teaching ourselves to value diversity in which difference is still the "Other"; it is to realize that we are ourselves the *product of difference* and not static beings, thus allowing ourselves to be located in the ever-shifting interstices of difference itself. In other words, it is an invitation to occupy, even if momentarily, unknown regions in which the Platonic pressure to seek resemblance and identity shrink, giving us glimpses of alternative possibilities of which the rhizoid space is one.

Thus, our philosophical project is to release us from representationalist thinking by embracing "the constantly changing sensible world of multiplicity and becoming" (Hayden, 1998, 133). Ethical experimentation with the manner in which boundaries come up around the sensible helps us to remain close to the relations of existence/difference themselves instead of relying too much on existing categories. Deleuze offers useful insight into the ways in which arbitrary composites or aggregates such as the human identity gain sovereignty through "despotic sign systems" and acquire reified boundaries through re-presentation. Therefore, examining sign systems earnestly begins the work of theory as praxis; experimenting with signs leads to an altered perception of the learning encounter as reciprocal presupposition, and a joint production of signs. And since signs are differentials, the productive power of positive difference comes into play. Each new sign or movement of difference poses a fresh problem for pedagogical investigation. Through our investigation of the sign, we reach the terrain of a signifying semiotics where language is a hand-to-hand combat with forces that occupy signs.

Further, Deleuze's concepts allow us to travel beyond our confining coordinates to a field of flux and indefinitude from which arise sensibilities and assemblages that are able to operate in new ways. From the point of view of meeting successfully the challenges of divergent spaces, this is of great importance; it validates differential experience not merely as an acknowledgment of an Other, but as the very processes through which reality is generated. Therefore, it frees us to look for and affirm curricular possibilities in unusual spaces that are generally overlooked. In particular, it helps us to see how the student and the learning encounter are fonts of curricular possibilities. Deleuze urges us to reach for the haecceities and singularities of our experience that are themselves multiplicities, with which to strive for new configurations of thought and feeling. From being transcendentally situated as the experiencer, there is the possibility of being inserted into the plane of experience itself. For example, when the categories around feelings break down, we enter an uncertain field of flux that is usually pathologized as schizophrenia by institutionalized psychoanalysis. But for Deleuze and Guattari, there is a creative schizoid process that gives access to an immanent state if "controlled schisis" can be maintained. Using Deleuzian concepts allows not just new curricular spaces but new ways of defining identity that are more compatible with irregular spaces.

Boundaries around curriculum and boundaries around identity are seen to open up when redescribed in Deleuzian terms of composites or aggregates. But for this to happen, we have to pay close attention to the internal differences within them. In other words, through theory as praxis the "badly analyzed composites" can be seen to be nothing other than exactly that—composites made up of traits, which can be destratified, and the singularities or microidentities released.

Once our sensibilities are opened up in a Deleuzian manner, life leaks out of the holes or fissures and forms multiplicities or rhizomes or plateaus of intensity with other composites. Entities lose "faciality" and become anonymous; boundaries lose their hard edges. The advantage of creating the image of ourselves as a rhizomatic multiplicity is that rhizomes have open borders and are constantly changing in architecture. They are nonhierarchical and more democratic. They are of the *order of the moss* and form plateaus of intensity, laterally strung out and contingent. Because of this flexibility they are eminently suitable for conceptualizing work in uncertain and irregular spaces and becomings.

In terms of the curriculum, they offer great flexibility, for rhizomes are connectivities; they ceaselessly attempt to establish new connections and interrupt molar formations. New connectivities generate vectors of virtuality and regions of surprise. They give us the freedom to consider new matter-thought compositions. In short, rhizomes have the possibility of reinserting life into the classroom because they search for intensity and cull it from difference; they show new ways of becoming, tapping from the existing life around them, bringing forth new concept-affect architecture.

As a first step toward such destratification, I offered the apprenticeship of the sign. The apprenticeship consists of four components: the adscension, the alloscension, the amnioscension, and the anascension. Each of these components performs a particular work of destratification, or conducts a move away from representation and resemblance. The apprenticeship is geared toward a moment-to-moment transformational awareness of the way sign regimes behave, and within that awareness, the rhizomatic possibilities of becoming different, of becoming-other together with other bodies, thoughts, and intensities. It teaches us to read everyday reality in a "foreign language" with a hesitancy and a stuttering, keeping in abeyance our everyday modes of apprehension.

The stuttering as creative hesitancy, a moment of generative flux in the curriculum, is another point I make in this work. In applying the fourfold analytical framework of the apprenticeship to the conversation between Carla and the teacher in chapter 4, we see how the possibility of such a moment arises but goes unheeded. If the attention were turned at that point to production of affect instead of being centered on meaning, it is conceivable that the entire situation could have evolved differently. In a different example, another teacher (JS) takes advantage of hesitancy or "stuttering" and begins to put to productive use the negative affect—in this case frustration and stress.

The next important point to come out of this work is the potency of the small interval. It makes use of the systems theoretical perspective of Francisco Varela in particular to support and clarify the Deleuzian emphasis on the small interval. The apprenticeship opens the door to dissident flows and *lines of disorientation*. It creates minor derailments from our gross identities, and contains the possibility of generating out of that disturbance minute, qualitatively different, space-time intervals. Small intervals can be very potent and theoretically powerful. The study of change must inevitably look into the small interval, since all transformation takes place in the confines of the infinitesimal as a passage to the limit. "Imperceptible rupture" and not "signifying break" thus becomes, in terms of praxis, the sites of rupture, allowing us to become aware of the fluxes that lie beneath our constituted selves. The signifying break or grand schemes of reform and change are rapidly taken over by territorializing forces, but an imperceptible rupture remains the hidden, unnoticed fault line that can allow what Britzman and Dippo (2000) have called "awful thoughts" or dissident movements to surface.

In terms of education, what this signifies is that the grand-scale reforms and large structural initiatives, although they may look impressive, are less important from the point of view of real change than the minor movements of disorientation and dissidence at the micropolitical level. For as Deleuze has observed, major signifying breaks are always captured by existing forces after a brief while and reinserted into the old spaces. This is what Deleuze calls "reterritorialization." Instead, smaller acts of rupture have greater possibility of escaping capture.

This brings us to yet another praxial move offered in this work— mapping affects. When we realize our multiplicities, there is a change in the image of ourselves from fixed identities to blocks of intensity or affect. When we enter a room or into an encounter, we do not enter as a preformed categorical entity, not even as a numerical multiplicity, that is, as several separate selves as some popular "postmodern" notions are apt to project, but as a *qualitative multiplicity*. This notion is central to Deleuze's thought. We enter in conjunction with the complex fields of indefinitude, fluxes and tendencies that have no particular shape and cannot be fitted into preexisting categories. In other words, we bring with us the complicated genetic abyssal shadows from which events, entities, statements, and thoughts arise as surface effects. These unformed singularities can form synthesis or assemblages with other such fields of force, whether human or not. It is precisely these unqualifiable fields of indefinitude that hold out the possibility of escaping our constituted selves or to "pour out of the holes of subjectivity," as Deleuze and Guattari put it (1987, 190). The case of E in the previous chapter was an illustration of the beginnings of such a deterritorialization, but without the necessary conceptual shift, E could not map her partial deterritorialization. Mapping here connotes not representing existing territory but creating a patchwork with other tendencies, traits, thoughts, and intensities.

To map affects therefore requires a combined concept-affect shift. In fact, in Deleuze, these are not ever fully separable. Concept and affect go together; conceptual architecture is closely connected to affective states, which in turn affects what it is possible to conceptualize. To create a map or an abstract diagram, sensation in the smallest interval must be watched in a pedagogic relationship, and like in E's case, sometimes a spillover occurs and a loss of sense of boundaries take us to the limit where feelings intermingle with other bodies resulting in the intensification of our powers of affecting and being affected. This is the construction of the diagram or the map of maps. The important claim here is that the pragmatics of the diagram can help prevent stress and burnout in teachers, that is, in those who are willing to experiment with the apprenticeship, by inserting the experimenter in a plane of immanence through minor destratifications.

This work of controlled schisis that I have described here must proceed with a lot of caution and careful experimentation. Desubjectification and the attempt to place the body in direct relation with the flows of other bodies by working past the naturalized organic unity does not imply a complete loss of all sense of cohesion and integration: "You have to keep enough of the organism for it to reform each dawn; and you have to keep small supplies of significance and subjectification, if only to turn them against their own systems when the circumstances demand it…and you have to keep small rations of subjectivity in sufficient quantity to enable you to…[m]imic the strata. You don't reach the plane of consistency by wildly destratifying" (Deleuze and Guattari, 1987, 160–61). In other words, it is neither possible nor desirable to fully deterritorialize the apparent organic unity of the entity; for strategic purposes, we have to maintain certain outward stratifications. Instead, the way to go about it is through minor destratifications and small intensifications, changes of velocity, retarding flows here and intensifying it there.

I have described this work as fieldwork in philosophy, in that it is a theoretical mode of analysis that nevertheless pays close attention to the complexities and dynamics of the educational encounter. It puts philosophy to work in a true Deleuzian fashion. I have tried to use philosophy to interrogate the lived experience of curriculum and thereby find new possibilities of action. In the case of teacher stress, it involved replacing the one-sided analysis of what happens to the teacher, usually found in mainstream literature, to the more complex one of theorizing the pedagogical encounter itself.

The shift from transcendence to immanence implies a renunciation of a priori, transcendent categories in terms of which change usually is sought. The transcendent is "paradigmatic, projective, hierarchical, and referential" (Deleuze and Guattari, 1987, 89), whereas immanence is the *jouissance* of difference and movement. Instead of the transcendent, which blocks movement and becoming, we construct a plane of immanence or of teacher becoming from within, through cautious experimentation and our eye on differential movements in small intervals. According to Deleuze, this is perhaps "the supreme act of philosophy," the task of showing the plane of immanence. The plane of immanence is not given but is constructed piece by piece even as we take our place in it, and it is subversive to domination and oppression. Deleuze (1995) remarks: "It is not immediately clear why immanence is so dangerous, but it is. It engulfs sages and gods. [For] immanence is immanent only to itself...and leaves nothing to which it could be immanent" (45). Immanence flattens authority structures and all transcendent claims to truth; it fills the dimensions with a *jouissance* or ecstasy of difference.

Finally, we must address the inevitable—the question of the concrete. Does this book, for instance, tell us what to do on Monday morning? Perhaps not, but what it attempts to do is to reconstitute "Monday morning" for us, so that it does not arrive all at once in its molar splendor. To put it differently, when our transcendental identities encounter other unified categories such as Monday mornings, the meeting of the two stratified unities may not produce a pleasant synthesis. What I have attempted throughout the book, and under different guises, is to shift our focus from macroscopic categories such as teacher, student, curriculum, or even Monday, and the problem of how to deal with them, to the constitutive differences and singularities that can be recomposed once we are in contact with the unsaid of the stated, the unthought of thought, and in general the forces that occupy signs and overcode differential experience, moving at all times toward a pragmatics of local formations.

What happens as a result of such experimentation is that 'Monday morning' never arrives, which is not to say we disappear in the void, but it does not arrive as a solidly oppressive order-word. As we enter our qualitative multiplicities, these differentiating series find many points of resonance with each other, and new points of communication arise. What allows these, or any two heterogeneous series to communicate with one another is the "dark precursor," or a second order differential—the difference of the differences—that has little to do with the original series but is able to oscillate to produce combinations. In other words, we imperceptibly enter, and become situated in the very plane from which an abstraction such as a category arises. Thus situated, we can combine with the singularities of a Monday morning in different ways to find new solutions.

Also, we must realize that the book is in one frame, and the category called 'Monday mornings' belongs to a different frame. As observers, we are able to see both frames simultaneously, and this is where part of the confusion arises. As Maturana and Varela would say, we move from one frame to another without acknowledging the move. Instead, if we lingered, say, in the book's frame, it would help us to do the necessary work or gather the force of insight necessary for deterritorializing the category called Monday mornings, resulting in a succession of independent durations that combine with our traits, and those of curricular material, to produce unique, and infinitely variegated, pedagogical moments—the construction of a plane of continual variation in which categories lose their transcendental image.

Finally, when molar categories are dismantled or deterritorialized, and assemblages return to the molecular, however briefly, before forming new categories, there is a force that is released that may be described as binding energy, a sudden liberatory intensity, a moment of what Deleuze might call *pure acceleration*. It allows us to confront whatever it is that we have to face, not from the known but from the unknown, a clear, darting line that, when we do the necessary hard work to stay on it, makes for a creative response. One could perhaps go so far as to say, and Deleuze does suggest this in several places, that staying on this line changes the very synaptic arrangements in the brain, since the concepts that we are dealing with are, each of them, a vector, or the point of application of a force that changes the image of thought, and along with that the "reality" we must deal with.

This continual and subtle transformation, if we are willing to do the necessary experimentation on ourselves, aligns us with some key cartographic elements for navigation on an altered plane: reciprocal presupposition, resonance, heterogeneity, progressive differentiation, plateaus of intensity, plane of composition, microintervals of affect, desire as production, and lines of acceleration, among others. Besides, the coordinates of the body on this plane are latitude and longitude—relations of transformation and relations of potentiality. The praxiological use of these concepts and constructs changes the image of thought.

In closing, I will quote Deleuze (1990) about ways of reading a book:

There are, you see, two ways of reading a book: you either see it as a box with something inside and start looking for what it signifies...Or there's the other way: you see the book as a little non-signifying machine. This second way of reading is intensive: something comes through or it doesn't. There's nothing to explain, nothing to understand, nothing to interpret. *It's like plugging into an electric circuit.* (8) (emphasis added)

Deleuzian concepts are "little non-signifying machines"; it is a mistake to try to see them in terms of mere signification, for the signifier leads us back to Oedipalized or controlled territory. Instead, what we must do is plug into these concepts or tiny "circuits" that have a destratifying charge of their own in any encounter, and see what they do mutually, if they do anything. We must experiment with them incessantly, and find out how, and if, they operate on our intensities and how the intensities operate on them. For Deleuze, a book is a tool box, but of a Borgesian kind, where the tools become, one by one, the very parts they were supposed to be working on, not as in an assimilation but a disjunctive synthesis, for they produce a difference and never the Same.

References

Abel, M. and Sewell, J. (1999). Stress and burnout in rural and urban secondary school teachers. *The Journal of Educational Research, 92* (5), 287–93.

Agar, M. (1980). *The professional stranger: An informal introduction to ethnography.* New York: Academic Press.

Bakhtin, M. (1981). *The dialogic imagination: Four essays.* Austin: University of Texas.

Bains, P. (2002). Subjectless subjectivities. In Brian Massumi (ed.). *A shock to thought: Expression after Deleuze and Guattari.* New York: Routledge.

Bateson, G. (1991). *A sacred unity: Further steps to an ecology of mind.* New York: Harper Collins.

Bauman, Z. (1992). *Intimations of postmodernity.* New York: Routledge.

Beckett, S. (1994). *Waiting for Godot.* New York: Grove Press.

Beller, J. L. (1998). Cinema, perception, and space. In Eleanor Kaufman and Kevin Heller (eds.). *Deleuze and Guattari: New mappings in politics, philosophy and culture* Minneapolis: University of Minnesota Press.

Bernstein, B. (1996) *Pedagogy, symbolic control, and identity: Theory, research, critique.* London: Taylor and Francis.

Best, S. and Kellner, D. (1991). *Postmodern theory.* New York: Guilford Press.

Blake, N., Smeyers, P. (1998). *Thinking again: Education after postmodernism.* Connecticut: Bergin & Garvey.

Boice, R. (1993). Writing blocks and tacit knowledge. *The Journal of Higher Education, 64* (Jan./Feb.), 19–54.

Borg, M. and Riding, R. (1993). Teacher stress and cognitive style. *The British Journal of Educational Psychology, 63* (June), 271–86.

Bourdieu, P. (1990). *In other words: Essays towards a reflexive sociology.* Stanford: Stanford University Press.

Boyle, G. et al. (1995). A structural model of the dimensions of teacher stress. *The British Journal of Educational Psychology, 65,* 49–67.

Britzman, D. (1986). Cultural myths in the making of a teacher. *Harvard Educational Review, 56* (4), 442–55.

———. (1998). *Lost subjects, contested objects: Toward a psychoanalytic theory of learning.* New York: SUNY Press.

———. (2002). The death of curriculum? In William Doll and Noel Gough (eds.). *Curriculum Visions.* New York: Peter Lang.

Britzman, D. P. & Dippo, D. (1998). Toward an academic framework for thinking about teacher education. *Teaching Education, 9* (1), 15–26.

———. (2000). On the future of awful thoughts in teacher education. *Teaching Education, 11* (1), 31–37.

Buchanan, I. (2000). *Deleuzism: A metacommentary.* Durham, NC: Duke University Press.

Byrne, J. J. (1998). Teacher as hunger artist: Burnout, its causes, effects, and remedies *Contemporary Education, 69* (2), 86–91.

Canetti, E. (1984). *Crowds and power.* Carol Stewart (Trans.). New York: Viking.

Cherryholmes, C. (1988). *Power and criticism: Poststructural investigations in education.* New York: Teachers College Press.

Cicourel, A. V. (1963). *The educational decision-makers.* Indianapolis: Bobbs Merrill & Co.

Conway, D. W. (1997). Tumbling dice: Gilles Deleuze and the economy of repetition. In K. A. Pearson (ed.). *Deleuze and philosophy: The difference engineer.* New York: Routledge.

Davis, B. et al. (2000). *Engaging minds: Learning and teaching in a complex world.* Mahwah, NJ: Lawrence Erlbaum Associates.

Deleuze, G. (1968/1994). *Difference and repetition.* Paul Patton (Trans.). New York: Columbia University Press.

———. (1972). *Proust and signs.* New York: George Braziller.

———. (1977). Intellectuals and power: A conversation between Michel Foucault and Gilles Deleuze. In Donald Bouchard (ed.). *Michel Foucault, Language, Counter-memory, Practice: Selected essays and interviews.* Ithaca, NY: Cornell University Press.

———. (1983). *Nietzsche and philosophy.* New York: Columbia University Press.

———. (1985). *Cinema 1: The movement image.* Minneapolis: University of Minnesota Press.

———. (1988a). *Spinoza: Practical philosophy.* San Francisco: City Lights.

———. (1988b). *Foucault.* Sean Hand (Trans.). Minneapolis: University of Minnesota Press.

———. (1990a). *Expressionism in philosophy: Spinoza.* Martin Joughin (Trans.). New York: Zone Books.

———. (1990b). *The logic of sense.* New York: Columbia University Press.

———. (1993). *The Deleuze Reader.* C. Boundas (Ed.). New York: Columbia University Press.

———. (1995). *Negotiations.* New York: Columbia University Press.

———. (1997). *Essays critical and clinical.* Minneapolis: University of Minnesota Press.

———. (1998). Having an idea in cinema: On the cinema of Straub-Huillet. In Eleanor Kaufman and Kevin Heller (eds.). *Deleuze and Guattari: New mappings in politics, philosophy and culture.* Minneapolis: University of Minnesota Press.

Deleuze, G. and Guattari, F. (1983a). *On the line.* New York: Columbia University Press.

———. (1983b). *Anti-Oedipus: Capitalism and schizophrenia.* Minneapolis: University of Minnesota Press.

———. (1986). *Nomadology: The war machine.* New York: Columbia University Press.

———. (1987). *A thousand plateaus: Capitalism and schizophrenia.* Brian Massumi (Trans.). Minneapolis: University of Minnesota Press.

———. (1994). *What is philosophy?* Hugh Tomlinson (Trans.). New York: Columbia

University Press.

Deleuze, G. and Parnet, C. (1987). *Dialogues*. Hugh Tomlinson and B. Habberjam (Trans.). New York: Columbia University Press.

Derrida, J. (1970). Structure, sign, and play in the discourse of the human sciences. In R. Macksey (ed.). *The structuralist controversy*. Baltimore: Johns Hopkins University Press.

Doll, W. (1999). Conversing with "the other." *Journal of Curriculum Theorizing, 15* (3), 83–89.

———. (2002). Ghosts and the curriculum. In W. Doll and N. Gough (eds.). *Curriculum visions*. New York: Peter Lang.

Eco, U. (1980). *The name of the rose*. New York: Harcourt Brace & Co.

Fendler, L. (1999). Making trouble: Prediction, agency and critical intellectuals. In T. Popkewitz and L. Fendler (eds.). *Critical theories in education: Changing terrains of knowledge and politics*. New York: Routledge.

Foucault, M. (1977). Nietzsche, genealogy, history. In D. F. Bouchard (ed.) *Language, counter-memory, practice: Selected essays and interviews*. New York: Cornell University Press.

———. (1979). *Discipline and punish*. Alan Sheridan (Trans.). New York: Vintage.

———. (1983). Introduction. In G. Deleuze and F. Guattari. *Anti-Oedipus*. Minneapolis: University of Minnesota Press.

———. (1984). *The Foucault Reader*. Paul Rabinow (ed.). New York: Pantheon Books.

———. (1988). *The care of the self: The history of sexuality, Vol. 3*. New York: Vintage Books.

———. (1994). *Ethics, subjectivity, truth*. Paul Rabinow (ed.). New York: New Press.

Friedman, I. (1995). Student behavior patterns leading to teacher burnout. *Journal of Educational Research, (88)* 5, 281–89.

Giroux, H. (2000). Postmodern education and disposable youth. In Peter Trifonas (ed.). *Revolutionary Pedagogies: Cultural politics, instituting education, and the discourse of theory*. New York: Routledgefalmer

Greene, M. (1973). *Teacher as stranger: Educational philosophy for the modern age*. Belmont, CA: Wadsworth Publishing Co.

Grosz, E. (1994a). A thousand tiny sexes. In Constantin Boundas and Dorothea Olkowski (eds.). *Gilles Deleuze and the theatre of philosophy*. New York: Routledge.

———. (1994b). *Volatile bodies: Towards a corporeal feminism*. Sydney: Allen and Unwin.

Grumet, M. (1988). *Bitter Milk: Women and teaching*. Amherst: University of Massachusetts Press.

Guattari, F. (1984). *Molecular revolution: Psychiatry and politics*. Rosemary Sheed (Trans.). New York: Penguin.

———. (1995). La Borde: A clinic unlike any other. In Sylvère Lotringer (ed.). *Chaosophy*. New York: Semiotext(e).

Hardt, M. (1993). *Gilles Deleuze: An apprenticeship in philosophy*. Minneapolis: University of Minnesota Press.

———. (1998). The withering of civil society. In Eleanor Kaufman and Kevin Heller (eds.). *Deleuze and Guattari: New mappings in politics, philosophy and culture*.

Minneapolis: University of Minnesota Press.

Hargreaves, A. (1994). *Changing teachers, changing times: teachers' work and culture in the postmodern age*. New York: Teachers College Press.

Hartley, D. (1997). *Re-schooling society*. Washington, D C: The Falmer Press.

Hayden, P. (1998). *Multiplicity and becoming: The pluralist empiricism of Gilles Deleuze*. New York: Peter Lang.

Hlebowitsh, P. S. (2000). *Radical curriculum theory reconsidered: A historical approach*. New York: Teachers college Press.

Irigaray, L. (1985). *This sex which is not one*. Ithaca, NY: Cornell University Press.

Jardine, A. (1985). *Gynesis: Configurations of woman and modernity*. Ithaca, NY: Cornell University Press.

Kaufman, E. (1998). Introduction. In Eleanor Kaufman and Kevin Heller (eds.). *Deleuze and Guattari: New mappings in politics, philosophy and culture*. Minneapolis: University of Minnesota Press.

Kliebard, H. M. (1992). *Forging the American curriculum*. London: Routledge.

Latour, B. (1993). *We have never been modern*. Cambridge, MA: Harvard University Press.

Lesko, N. (1995). The "leaky needs" of school-aged mothers: An examination of US programs and policies. *Curriculum Inquiry, (25)*, 2.

Levi Strauss, C. (1969). *The raw and the cooked*. J. Weightman and D. Weightman (Trans.). New York: Harper & Row.

Liston, D. and Zeichner, K. M. (1996). *Culture of teaching*. Mahwah, NJ: L. Erlbaum Associates.

Luhmann, N. (1989). *Ecological communication*. John Bednarz (Trans.). Chicago: University of Chicago Press.

———. (1990). The cognitive program of constructivism and a reality that remains unknown. In W. Krohn et al. (eds.). *Selforganization: Portrait of a scientific revolution*. Dordrecht: Kluwer.

Maslach, C. (1993). Burnout: A multidimensional perspective. In W. B. Schaufeli (ed.). *Professional Burnout: Recent developments in theory and research*. Washington, DC: Taylor & Francis.

Massumi, B. (1992). *A user's guide to capitalism and schizophrenia: Deviations from Deleuze and Guattari*. Cambridge, MA: MIT Press.

———. (1995). The autonomy of affect. *Cultural Critique, 31, (fall 1995)*.

———. (2002). Introduction. In Brian Massumi (ed.). *A shock to thought: Expression after Deleuze and Guattari*. New York: Routledge.

Maturana, H. (1990). Science and daily life: The ontology of scientific explanations. In W. Krohn et al. (eds.). *Selforganization: Portrait of a scientific revolution*. Dordrecht: Kluwer.

Maturana, H. and Varela, F. J. (1998). *The tree of knowledge: The biological roots of human understanding*. Boston: Shambhala.

McCarthy, C. and Dimitriadis, G. (2000a). All-consuming identities: Race and the pedagogy of resentment in the age of difference. In Peter Trifonas (ed.). *Revolutionary Pedagogies: Cultural politics, instituting education and the discourse of theory*. New York: RoutledgeFalmer.

_____. (2000b). Globalizing pedagogies: Power, resentment, and the renarration of difference. In R. Mahalingam and C. McCarthy (eds.). *Multicultural curriculum: New directions for social theory, practice, and policy.* New York: Routledge.

Meier, D. (1995). *The power of their ideas: Lessons for America from a small school in Harlem.* Boston: Beacon Press.

Molnar, A. (2002). The commercialization of America's schools. In W.E. Doll and N. Gough (eds.). *Curriculum visions.* New York: Peter Lang.

Murphy, T. S. (1998). Quantum ontology: A virtual mechanics of becoming. In Eleanor Kaufman and Kevin Heller (eds.). *Deleuze and Guattari: New mappings in politics, philosophy and culture.* Minneapolis: University of Minnesota Press.

National Commission on Teaching and America's Future. (1996). *Report of the Commission.* Washington DC: NCTAF.

Nietzsche, F. (1967). *On the genealogy of morals. Vol. I.* W. Kaufmann and R. J. Hollingdale (Trans.). New York: Random House.

Nietzsche, F. (1982). *Daybreak: Thoughts on the prejudices of morality.* R. J. Hollingdale (Trans.). Cambridge: Cambridge University Press.

Nietzsche, F. (1983). *Untimely meditations.* New York: Cambridge University Press.

North Central Regional Educational Lab (NCREL). (1998). *Milwaukee Public School District Innovative School Program: Final Report Addendum.* Oak Brook, IL: NCREL.

Olebe, M. (2001). Beginning teacher support and assessment program. *Teacher Education Quarterly 28* (1), 71–84.

Pearson, K. A. (1997). *Deleuze and philosophy: The difference engineer.* New York: Routledge.

Pinar, W. (1994). *Autobiography, politics, and sexuality: essays in curriculum theory (1972–1992).* New York: Peter Lang.

_____. (1995). *Understanding curriculum: An introduction to the study of historical and contemporary curriculum discourses.* New York: Peter Lang.

_____. (1998). *Curriculum: Toward new identities.* New York: Garland Publications.

_____. (2002) *The Internationalization of curriculum studies: A history and status report.* Paper presented at AAACS Conference, New Orleans.

Polya, G. (1957). *How to solve it: A new aspect of mathematical method.* Princeton, NJ: Princeton University Press.

Popkewitz, T. S. (1988). Educational reform: Rhetoric, ritual, and social interest. *Educational Theory 38* (1).

Rajchman, J. (1998). *Constructions.* Cambridge, MA: MIT Press.

_____. (2000). *The Deleuze Connections.* Cambridge, MA: MIT Press.

Ricouer, P. (1985). History as narrative practice. *Philosophy Today (fall 1985).*

Sanders, M. (2000). *Schooling students placed at risk: Research, policy, and practice.* Mahwah, NJ: L. Erlbaum Associates.

Saussure, F. de. (1959). *Course in general linguistics.* Charles Balley and Albert Reidlinger (eds.). New York: Philosophical Library.

Schwanitz, D. (1987). Systems theory and the environment of theory. In C. Koelb and V. Lokke (eds.). *The current in criticism: Essays on the present and future of literary theory.* W. Lafayette, IN: Purdue University Press.

Shukin, N. (2000). Deleuze and feminisms: Involuntary regulators and affective inhibitors. In Ian Buchanan and Claire Colebrook (eds.). *Deleuze and feminist theory*. Edinburgh: Edinburgh University Press.

Swaminathan, R. (forthcoming). *Epimeleia: An ethic of pedagogic care. Review of Research in Education*.

Taussig, M. (1993). *Mimesis and alterity: A particular history of the senses*. New York: Routledge.

Varela, F. (1992). *Ethical know-how: Action, wisdom, and cognition*. Stanford: Stanford University Press.

Vázquez, A. S. (1977). *The philosophy of praxis*. Atlantic Highlands, NJ: The Humanities Press.

Von Glasersfeld, E. (1987). *The construction of knowledge: Contribution to conceptual semantics*. Seaside, CA: Intersystems Publications.

Walkerdine, V. (1988). *The mastery of reason*. New York: Routledge.

Weisberg, J. and Sagie, A. (1999). Emotional burnout: Impact on intention to quit. *The Journal of Psychology, 133*(3), 333–9.

Weiss, E. and Weiss, S. (1999). Beginning teacher induction. *ERIC Digest*; Washington DC: ERIC; 1999–11–00.

Willis, P. (1977). *Learning to labour: How working class lads get working class jobs*. Farnborough, England: Saxon House.

Wolcott, H. (1994). *Transforming qualitative data*. London: Sage Publications.